Growing Garlic
A Complete Guide To Growing, Harvesting & Using Garlic

Jason Johns

Visit me at www.OwningAnAllotment.com for gardening tips and advice or follow me at www.YouTube.com/OwningAnAllotment for my video diary and tips. Join me on Facebook at www.Facebook.com/OwningAnAllotment.

If you have enjoyed this book, please leave a review on Amazon. I read each review personally and the feedback helps me to continually improve my books.

As someone who has bought this book on Amazon you are entitled to a free download of the Kindle version. This will enable you to get the full color book in electronic format. Unfortunately I have to publish these books in black and white in order to make them affordable due to the high cost of color printing. Please download this from Amazon; you can read it on a Kindle or any tablet, cell phone or computer with the free Kindle Reader installed from your app store.

© 2017 Jason Johns

All rights reserved.

TABLE OF CONTENTS

What is Garlic & Why People Love It..................*1*
The History of Garlic..................*6*
Different Types of Garlic..................*9*
Ideal Garlic Growing System..................*13*
Growing Garlic..................*17*
Fertilizing, Mulching & Watering..................*24*
Harvesting, Curing, Storing & Preserving..................*26*
Diseases & Pests..................*33*
Companion Planting..................*39*
Therapeutic Uses of Garlic..................*42*
Growing Garlic for Profit..................*52*
Cooking with Garlic..................*56*
Other Members of the Onion Family..................*65*
Endnote..................*72*
About Jason..................*74*
Other Books By Jason..................*76*
Want More Inspiring Gardening Ideas?..................*80*

What is Garlic & Why People Love It

Garlic is a wonderful plant loved for both its medicinal and culinary uses. Popular for thousands of years around the world, it is enjoyed today in a wide range of cooking. It's a hard plant to define ... is it an herb or a spice?

Related to onions, leeks, chives and shallots it is a member of the lily family. With an intense and unique flavor plus its well-known aroma, it is a staple of virtually every cuisine.

Garlic grows underground as a bulb with long green shoots coming up from the ground whilst the bulb expands into the cloves we know and love to cook with. Few people eat raw garlic as your breath will be particularly pungent afterwards; most people cook garlic to add flavor to dishes. Rarely the main ingredient in cooking, though occasionally whole roasted cloves are eaten as the roasting mellows the flavor.

It's very easy to grow garlic at home, but the long growing season puts many people off. However, home grown garlic stores well and you can grow some very interesting varieties with unusual flavors that you cannot buy in the shops.

Garlic, or Allium Sativum to give it its Latin name, does grow in the wild. There are a wide variety of wild garlics that grow in different countries around the world. In the UK, there is both wild garlic and Jack O' The Hedge, which are wild plants (commonly thought of as weeds) which grow in profusion with garlic flavored leaves, one of which is pictured below. In warmer climates where garlic is naturalized, the garlic varieties that grow into bulbs can be found.

In North America, there is wild or crow garlic, Allium Vineaele as well as wild or meadow garlic, Allium Canadense. These grow in fields and hedgerows, being common in most states. Elephant garlic, Allium Ampeloprasum, is not a true garlic but a wild leek. Pearl or Solo garlic which is a single clover garlic is native to China's Yunnan province, and rarely seen in the West.

There are a lot of different types of garlic around, though most cultivars represent just a few of the more popular varieties. You can find heritage garlic bulbs, which are the less common varieties that are often very interesting to grow and eat.

There are two subspecies of garlic; hardneck garlic (Allium Sativum var. Ophioscorodon) and softnecked garlic (Allium Sativum var.Sativum). Hardnecked varieties include the porcelain garlic, purple striped garlic and rocambole garlic. Softnecked varieties include creole, silver skin and artichoke garlic.

Garlic can be grown in almost any climate as it is very tolerant of a wide variety of temperatures. In colder climates garlic thrives, usually planted about six weeks before the soil freezes in October or November. Garlic is a hardy plant and will survive being covered with snow providing the clove is planted deep enough.

The nice thing about garlic is that you can grow it pretty much anywhere. It will grow in pots, in the soil, in hot climates and in cold climates. There are a huge variety in garlic bulbs, with a wide variation in flavor. Some are more intense than others plus depending on how you prepare it the flavor will vary.

Garlic is popular in cuisines from around the world and is a popular flavoring, though there are a small amount of people who are allergic to it. You are probably most familiar with it from Italian and French cuisine, where it is in almost every dish, though it is great flavoring in low calorie meals as it is virtually calorie free. A lot of diet dishes will be laced with garlic as it is an easy way to make a meal taste interesting.

Where you are in the world will influence the type of garlic you plant, as some varieties can be sensitive to the amount of daylight they get. In colder climates, you are typically growing a hardneck variety. In warmer areas, softneck garlic is more popular and will thrive.

Garlic is a massive commercial crop, though you should never plant garlic from the supermarket as you don't know it is disease free. China is the largest producer of garlic, account for almost 80% of the global output. Other major exporters of garlic include India, South Korea, Egypt and the United States, where Gilroy, California is touted as the "garlic capital of the world".

Not only does garlic add flavor to your cooking, but it is also immensely popular for its therapeutic qualities. A lot of research is underway into how garlic extracts can be used medicinally, with some of it proving extremely promising in treating a variety of diseases and conditions.

Having been used in traditional medicine for hundreds, if not thousands of years, garlic is known to have a wide range of medicinal properties, including:

- Boosting the immune system
- Lowering bad cholesterol levels
- Reducing blood pressure
- Powerful antioxidant and anti-aging properties
- Reducing the risk of blood clots
- Strong anti-fungal properties
- Powerful antibacterial agent

The familiar smell and taste of garlic comes from the sulfur compounds found in it, similar to those found in onions. Allicin is probably the best known of these as it boosts the immune system and slows down the activity of a wide range of bacteria and viruses. Garlic has been proven to be effective in killing a wide range of harmful bacteria, including salmonella, staphylococcus, E. coli and listeria, amongst others.

Garlic is high in a number of vital vitamins, including C and B6 plus essential trace elements such as calcium, selenium, copper and manganese. Its antibacterial properties are well known with Louis Pasteur confirming them during his research in the 1850's. In World War II the Russian army ran out of penicillin to treat its soldiers and turned to garlic instead, with it being referred to as the "Russian Penicillin". It was mixed into a paste and applied topically to wounds to prevent infection.

Research is underway into other health benefits of garlic, with it shown to reduce the risk of heart disease by lowering bad cholesterol levels. In a 1994 study by the University of Minnesota it was confirmed that eating garlic regularly together with fruits and vegetables reduced the risk of cancer by as much as 35%. More recent research indicates the sulfur compounds found in garlic can inhibit the growth of brain cancer cells.

Garlic is a very versatile plant and is well worth using in your cooking. It has many health benefits and a wonderful flavor. To get a bolder flavor from your garlic, mince or purée it, but add fine slivers of garlic for a subtle aroma. Whilst raw garlic gives you the most significant health benefits, it can have a negative impact on your social life. The pungent breath and body odor that comes from eating lots of garlic doesn't make it the most sociable of plants. However, cooked garlic doesn't have quite the same negative effect on your social life and still has numerous health benefits. Do expect people to know you've been eating garlic, as even cooking can't get rid of its distinctive after effects.

As you read this book you will learn everything you need to know to successfully grow garlic at home. You will learn the exact conditions garlic needs to grow and what pests and diseases may strike your plants. It is a wonderful plant to grow and even though it has a long growing season, it is worth it because it does store well. Freshly grown garlic has a wonderful taste and growing it yourself means you can grow the more unusual varieties that have much better flavors which you cannot find in the shops.

Enjoy growing your own garlic, but enjoy using it even more. It's a wonderful plant with a fantastic taste!

The History of Garlic

Garlic has a long and somewhat chequered history, seen as something fit for the gods and as something reviled and suitable only to be fed to pigs! For more than 5,000 years it has been used for everything from medicine to food to money to an aphrodisiac to a component in magic potions!

Garlic has protected medieval families from the evil eye when hung over a door, given courage to Greek warriors, protected maidens from evil nymphs and kept away vampires. Pendants made from garlic cloves have provided protection from bull's horns and local witches as well as warding off the Black Plague,

Rarely has one plant had so much mythology associated with it and been known to be such a vital ingredient in cookery.

In ancient Egypt garlic was extremely precious, being seen as a god and as a currency! Clay garlic bulbs have been found in tombs, though whether as currency or an offering to appease the gods is not known. It was used as both a food and as payment for the pyramid workforce. In fact, garlic was in such demand that there was strikes amongst the workforce when it was in short supply. There are only two recorded slave revolts in ancient Egypt and one of those was caused when the river Nile flooded and caused the garlic crop to fail!

Oddly enough, despite its popularity amongst the working classes, garlic was considered too common for the upper echelons of Egyptian society. Although the priests worshipped garlic and used it in their ceremonies, they would refrain from sullying their bodies by eating it.

The Egyptians weren't alone in considered garlic too pungent for the priesthood. In Greece, those who wanted to enter the sacred temple of Cybele had to pass a garlic breath test to gain entry! Those who passed were allowed in whilst those who did not were turned away.

In ancient India, the same applied; common people used garlic whilst the aristocracy avoided it because of the strong smell and its popularity amongst the lower classes. King Alfonso de Castille would cast knights who smelt of garlic out of his court for a week! In England, garlic was considered unsuitable for refined young ladies and any gentleman who wished to court them. Americans adopted the same attitude and it wasn't until the 1940's that garlic gained any popularity in the USA. Prior to this it was considered an ethnic ingredient, known by a variety of slang terms, many derogatory, including "Italian perfume".

Garlic has also been strongly believed to be an aphrodisiac and to inflame the passions. It has been, at various times in history, forbidden to widows, adolescents and to Tibetan monks. In Chinese medicine, it was prescribed to men who had issues with "intimacy" whilst grooms put cloves of garlic in their buttonholes to ensure their honeymoon went well. I don't think my wife would have been impressed if I had turned up to our wedding with some garlic instead of a carnation, but this is just one of the many associations this mystical plant has.

Throughout history garlic has been mentioned all over the world, with it being specifically recorded in ancient writings from Egypt, India, China and Greece, as well as being explicitly mentioned in the Quran, Bible and Talmud. Medicinally it was used by the Greeks, Chinese, Egyptians and Europeans. It was used to cure a wide variety of ailments from impotence to heart disease to the Black Plague!

There is quite a bit of debate over the origin of garlic as it is one of the oldest cultivated crops in the world. It is believed that it may well have been a native of central or Southern Asia or possibly southwest Siberia. Being such a popular plant it was carried all over the world by explorers and migrants, now growing wild in southern Europe and Italy. In his book, "Back to Eden" Jethro Kloss wrote that garlic has been used for as long as people have been eating food.

The name originates from an old Anglo-Saxon word, garleac, which means "spear leek". Since the 1990s, garlic consumption in the United States alone has tripled and there is in excess of 2.5 million acres given over to the cultivation of garlic!

Garlic has a rich history, being used all over the world for everything from medicine to protection to good luck. Having waxed and waned in favor, it is now a very popular plant used in cuisines across the world. As you read this book you will learn about the wide variety of different types of garlic and how to grow it. You'll discover the many different varieties other than the few found in stores.

DIFFERENT TYPES OF GARLIC

You may be forgiven for not realizing that there are different types of garlic as stores very rarely stock these different types. Garlic, like other vegetables, is selected for sale based on its ability to be transported and preserved, rather than flavor or any other qualities.

Softneck Garlic
This is the most commonly seen garlic in your local grocery store, with its name coming from the multiple layers of papery parchment covering the bulb and continuing up the neck which makes it ideal for braiding.

The papery skin is a bright or creamy white color and will usually have a large outer layer of cloves and sometimes smaller cloves inside these.

There are two common types of softneck garlic, and sub-varieties of these.

Silverskin Garlic

An easy to grow variety with a good, strong flavor plus it stores well, lasting for around a year when dried and stored correctly. There is a variety of silverskin called Creole which has a slight rose tint to the parchment and is particularly sought after in cooking.

Common varieties of silverskin garlic include:

- Chet's Italian Red
- Inchelium
- Kettle River Giant
- Polish White

Artichoke Garlic

This is a milder variety which has fewer cloves than silverskin, but they are larger with multiple, overlapping layers that can contain as many as 20 cloves. The outer layer is hard to peel and they are a white / cream color. It stores for around eight months and can have purple spots or streaks on the skin. This is often confused with a hardneck variety with purple coloring known as purple stripe garlic.

Some of the more popular artichoke garlic varieties are:

- Applegate
- California Early
- California Late
- Chamiskuri
- Early Red Italian
- Galiano
- Italian Late
- Italian Purple
- Inchelium Red
- Lorz Italian
- Polish Red
- Red Troch

Hardneck Garlic

Hardneck garlic varieties have a stalk that isn't flexible, unlike the softneck varieties. Typically, this variety will have a couple of inches of stalk sticking up from the bulb. When these varieties grow, they send up thin green stalks from the middle stalk which have a 360-degree curl and a swelling on the end. These are referred to as scrapes and inside the swelling (bulbil) there are over a hundred tiny cloves which are genetic clones of the main bulb.

Often referred to as flowers, they aren't really but shouldn't be left on the plant as they suck energy from the formation of the main bulb. If you leave the scrapes they will die back and fall over, spreading their seeds over the ground. These should be removed from the plant so it concentrates on producing the large bulb you want and they can be used in cooking.

Hardneck varieties are often much easier to peel than their softneck cousins.

There are three types of hardneck garlic commonly seen:

- Rocambole – with a rich taste, this variety peels easily and will typically have just a single set of cloves around the thick, woody stalk. It will store for around six months.
- Porcelain – similar to the previous variety in flavor, it will usually contain only four large cloves wrapped in the white papery parchment. This variety if often mistaken for elephant garlic because of the large cloves and stores for approximately eight months.
- Purple Stripe – this is by far the best variety for making baked garlic and there are a number of different purple stripe varieties. It is very distinctive with its bright purple streaks and will usually keep for around six months.

Elephant garlic is another variety grown by home gardeners. It has very large bulbs but a very mild flavor, making it ideal for people who do not like a strong garlic taste. Its taste is closer to that of a leek and it is not as useful medicinally as other garlic varieties.

Finding the Perfect Bulb
Choosing the right bulb is very important. You can buy the more common varieties in a lot of different stores around planting time (spring or fall) or you can buy the more unusual varieties online.

You are looking for bulbs that are:

- Completely dry
- Has plump and firm cloves
- Covered in lots of papery parchment

Avoid any cloves that are:

- Soft, spongy, shrivelled or crumbly
- Showing green shoots (means they are past their prime)

If you buy your garlic bulbs early in the season, then you will find they are fresh and good quality. Typically, buying them later in the season means many are past their prime and you must be more careful in choosing the right bulbs.

Ideal Garlic Growing System

Before planting garlic, it is important that you prepare the soil correctly. Determine whether you already have a good soil or whether you need to amend it. However, garlic is forgiving and will do well in almost any type of soil, so you can probably get away with growing garlic in almost any soil except the heaviest, waterlogged clay.

Garlic prefers a soil that is loose and drains well. A sandy loam is ideal but even in clay it will grow. Garlic, though, does not like growing when stood in water and will rot if the soil retains water too well. If you do have a clay soil, then build some raised beds or dig in sand and organic matter to help the soil drain better.

Clay also sticks to the papery outer skin of garlic, which makes it hard to clean the garlic and for it to store well. It can also make harvesting garlic difficult, particularly if the clay has hardened due to dry weather. If your soil has a lot of clay in, then ensure you use a hand fork to dig up your garlic and clean off as much soil as you can without wetting the bulb before you dry it.

Although garlic is fairly forgiving of soil conditions, getting the right conditions can make a huge difference not only in the crop you get but also in the health of your plants.

Garlic likes the soil pH to be between 6.0 and 7.5, which you can measure with a pH tester, available online or from garden stores. If your soil is too far from this ideal pH, then you need to amend the soil so it is within this range.

There are not a lot of leaves on garlic so you could be forgiven for thinking that garlic doesn't need a lot of nitrogen, which promotes leaf growth. Particularly during its initial growth phase, it will need high levels of nitrogen so benefits from some organic manure being added to the bed.

Like other plants, garlic does need phosphorus, which promotes healthy root growth, which will come from any good organic compost or manure. Potassium is also useful, which you will find in the manures you use.

One element garlic does benefit from is sulfur (sulphur), which is directly linked to both the healing properties of the plant and its flavours. Sprinkle some gypsum over the beds once the plants are forming leaves to add this vital element.

You should be careful when adding manure as adding fresh manure will burn the roots and the leaves of the plant. Avoid adding manure too close to harvest time as you don't want the residue on the bulbs.

Chicken manure is great for garlic and has very high levels of nitrogen. This is available fresh if you know someone who keeps chickens or you can buy it as a pelleted manure. If buying pellets, then choose organic as you know there are no harmful chemicals in it. You scatter the manure on top of the bed or dig it in according to the manufacturer's instructions. Gradually it breaks down, releasing nutrients into the soil.

Horse manure is another good source of nitrogen, but it needs to be well rotted to really be of any use. Let the manure rot down for 6 to 9 months before applying it, or dig it into the bed a couple of months before planting. Fresh manure is hot and this can damage plants, stunting growth or even killing them.

Green manures, such as alfalfa, are also great ways to amend the soil. You can grow these or you can buy alfalfa pellets. You simple plant the seeds, let the plant grow and then after a few weeks of growth dig it into the soil. As the plants rot down they release beneficial nutrients into the soil. This is a great way of amending heavy clay soils and breaking them up.

Another good feed for your garlic plants is compost, comfrey or nettle tea. These are easy to make and are high in nutrients. The liquid is diluted in water and watered on to your plants. A lot of home growers swear these teas are their secret sauce for prolific crops because it also acts as a foliar feed.

When planting garlic, it likes to spread its roots out, so loosen up the soil and make sure there are no obstructions such as rocks or branches. The roots do not go deep, so you only need to really clear the top few inches of the bed. Some people reckon sieving the soil is the best thing to do, but not everyone is willing to go to that much effort.

Making Compost Teas

These teas are very easy to make, though they are extremely smelly, so best not done near a door. They are nutrient dense and very beneficial for your plants so are worth making. Nettle and comfrey tea are made from what are effectively weeds, so gardener's get a certain satisfaction of using weeds like this to benefit their plants.

Which tea you choose to make is entirely up to you and depends on what is available in your area. Compost tea is very easy as most of us have access to compost but nettle and comfrey tea are renowned for being extremely beneficial to plants and well worth the effort to make.

Compost Tea

Compost tea is easy to make and is a good food for your plants, and one garlic will benefit from.

1. Fill a bucket a third full of good quality compost (home-made or store bought)
2. Top the bucket up with water until it is almost full
3. Cover and leave for 3 or 4 days, stirring occasionally
4. Strain through cheesecloth or another porous material into another bucket
5. Put the solids back on your compost pile
6. Dilute with water at a 10:1 ratio before using
7. Use straight away direct on the soil around your plants
8. Alternatively, use as a foliar spray by adding a dash of vegetable oil so the tea sticks to the leaves

Comfrey Tea

Comfrey tea is a good liquid feed and a great way to get your own back on the weeds by using them for the benefit of your plants. It makes for a good tomato food.

You will need a large bucket. Fill a hessian bag with comfrey leaves so that it about half fills your bucket. These are best when they have spent a day wilting and you roughly chop or tear them. If you don't have any hessian bags, use some pantyhose (tights) or an old pillow case.

Fill the bucket with water and push the bag down into the water to get any air bubbles out. Cover the bucket and leave it for between two and four weeks, the cooler the weather, the longer you leave it.

Now, this liquid is going to stink to high heaven, so you need to make sure it's nowhere that is going to upset anyone and it will attract flies if you leave it uncovered. Basically, put it as far away from people as possible!

When you are ready to use it, strain it off. A lot of people will make their comfrey tea in a container with a tap on the bottom to make it easier to get the tea out.

Dilute this before use, a ratio of 10:1 is good. It is best applied direct to the roots and is particularly good for tomatoes, though bell peppers, chillies, cucumbers and other vegetables will appreciate this feed. Garlic will like this, though aim for the base of the plant rather than the leaves.

Nettle Tea
This is another great fertilizer for your garlic and other plants, being another good way to get your own back on the weeds in your garden. You will need some nettles, a bucket, a brick and some water to make this plant food.

You will need about three quarters of a bucket of nettles, when pressed down. Young stems are best, and bruise the leaves and stems before adding the water in order to get more nutrients out of them. Remember to wear gloves as these sting and are unpleasant!

Put the nettles in your bucket and then put the brick or other large stone on top of them to weigh them down. Fill the container with water, cover and leave in a corner somewhere out of the way as it will smell.

After three or four weeks, it should be ready to use. Dilute at a ratio of 10:1 with water before use. This can be made throughout the year and really gives your plants a boost!

GROWING GARLIC

Garlic grows very well anywhere from a Mediterranean climate to a British or Canadian climate. It is a relatively easy crop to grow that doesn't require a great deal of attention.

You usually plant garlic in the fall months as the cold during winter helps the bulbs to form. Cloves planted at this time tend to produce larger bulbs. Garlic can also be planted in the spring, but the bulbs tend to be smaller. Garlic can be ready to harvest any time from May through to about August, depending on the variety planted and the size you want the bulbs to grow to.

When the plant's foliage turns yellow and starts to wilt it is time to harvest the garlic. You can eat them fresh or dry them and store them for use later in the year.

Which variety you decide to plant is entirely up to you, though the softneck varieties are far easier to grow and stores very well. The hardneck varieties don't store as well but produce larger cloves and many garlic lovers claim this type cannot be beaten for flavor.

Always make sure that you buy a variety that is suited to the climate you live in. If you buy them from a physical shop, then you will find the varieties sold are usually varieties that will grow in your area. Although you may be tempted to plant garlic from a supermarket, I don't recommend it. This garlic is not certified as disease free and may not grow at all in your climate.

Fall Planting
Some garlic varieties are best planted as winter draws in, ready for harvest the following summer. These are easy to plant and grow from sets.

Garlic prefers a sunny site with well-drained soil. Prepare the soil well, ensuring the soil is not too acidic by adding lime if necessary. Digging in organic matter or horticultural (sharp) sand can help make the soil drain better. If your soil is particularly bad, then build a raised bed. This doesn't need to be deep, 4 to 6 inches is plenty and then fill it with the perfect soil. You can even grow garlic in containers, but you need to ensure there is adequate drainage, so drill holes in the bottom of the container as required.

Garlic cloves are planted about 6" (15cm) apart and 2-3" (5-7cm) deep with the pointy end of the clove facing upwards. In a clay soil, plant the cloves slightly shallower. Water in well after planting.

Maintaining the bed is very easy, use your hoe to keep weeds down, being careful to avoid damaging the bulbs. Covering the bed in black plastic and planting through it works very well and is a good way to keep the weeds down. Garlic does not like competition, so keeping the weeds down is essential for healthy plants.

Feeding Fall Garlic

How you feed your garlic will depend on how well you prepared your bed. If you dug in a lot of manure to increase nutrient levels, then your plants need less fertilizer throughout the year. If you didn't prepare the soil, you need to give your plants a bit more fertilizer. Check the manufacturer's instructions and add 50% for soil that hasn't been prepared in advance.

Watering Fall Garlic

The manure you have dug into the soil will help it retain moisture, which garlic likes. Once you plant your garlic, water it in and then do not water it again until spring. There should be plenty of water coming from rain over the winter months and if garlic gets waterlogged then the newly planted cloves can rot.

Garlic is particularly susceptible to fungal diseases which love wet leaves, so always water directly to the soil, avoiding getting any water on the leaves. When the foliage starts to die back, stop watering completely.

Harvesting and Storing

When the leaves start to yellow and wither, usually anywhere from early to mid-summer, lift the bulbs carefully using a fork and dry in a light, airy environment, such as a greenhouse.

In a warm summer, allow to dry for a couple of weeks, but if the summer is duller then leave them for a month. Once dry, remove the leaves, composting them, and store in a cool dry place until required.

Fall garlic is susceptible to leek rust, leek moth, onion white rot and split bulbs, which occurs when you harvest too later.

Spring Planting Garlic

Some varieties of garlic can be planted in spring for a later summer harvest. This is great for when you realize you forgot to plant garlic and gives you winter to prepare beds for the spring. These suffer from the same problems as fall planted garlic but in areas with harsh winters can mean your garlic survives the colder months! Of course, if you live in a colder area then you can fleece your garlic to protect the leaves from harsh frosts and encourage them to grow.

With a shorter growing season these are very popular with gardener's and are very easy to grow.

Spring planted garlic likes the same soil conditions as fall planted garlic. They are planted 6" apart, 2-3" deep and in rows of 12" (30cm) apart.

Feeding and watering is the same as for fall planting, as is harvesting. The only difference really is when you plant the bulbs.

I have tried growing both varieties and found that in my area the damp winters encourage fungal growth and rust on the leaves which killed my crop. The spring planting varieties work best here because the leaves are not getting soggy over winter. Which works best in your area will depend on your climate and the weather over winter. Don't worry if you get snow as I have had garlic covered in snow and it has still produced bulbs the following year. In colder climates, you may want to cover your crop with fleece to protect it from the harshest weather, but it is surprisingly hardy.

Buying Bulbs

Where you buy your bulbs from will depend on what type of bulbs you are after and where you live. I usually buy mine from a local store as they have the varieties I require in stock and are easily available.

Specialist varieties are not stocked in stores, they tend to have more generic varieties, so if you are after something different then you will need to order it online. Check where the bulbs are coming from because if they are coming from outside of your country then you may have issues getting them through customs.

If you are buying the bulbs in person, then squeeze the bulbs before you buy them. They should be firm. If they are soft, then don't buy them as they are rotting and past their best. Likewise, if they brittle and crumble when you squeeze them, they are also not viable as they have dried too much.

After being in storage for a while the garlic bulbs will start to send out green shoots as they try to grow. These should also be avoided as there is a chance the bulb has expended its energy in producing the shoots and will not grow when planted in soil.

The earlier in the season you buy your garlic, the more likely it will be viable. It is only when you get towards the end of the season and are buying what's left on the shelf that you have problems finding good quality bulbs.

When to Plant

Check the packet of the garlic you bought for when you plant it. It will either be a spring or fall (autumn) planting variety. Plant according to the instructions on the packet.

If you are not planting your garlic immediately, then store it in a cool, dry and dark environment until you are ready to put it in the ground.

Garlic is planted 2-3" deep and 6" apart in rows spaced at 12". In clay soils, you do not plant as deep. You can dig out a small hole or push the garlic directly into the soil. You want the tip of each clove to be about 1"

below the surface of the soil.

Personally, I lay the garlic out on the ground with the correct spacing and then adjust it if I need to fit in a couple of extra bulbs. Planting guides are just that, guides, and if you are using raised beds with high quality soil you can get away with a closer spacing, but must still ensure there is sufficient room for air to circulate around the leaves. Giant garlic varieties require more space than normal varieties.

If the weather is particularly bad, then you may want to wait until the weather improves slightly before you plant it. You don't want to plant into a waterlogged soil which will cause the bulbs to rot.

Growing Guide

Anyone with a heavy, clay soil that retains water is best starting their garlic off in modules in the fall months rather than plant direct in the soil. The garlic is then overwintered in a cold frame to protect it from getting waterlogged and planted out in the spring as the soil dries out.

Partially fill the cells of your module tray with a good quality compost and put one clove in each module. Cover with compost and water in, making sure the compost is moist but not wet. Store in a cold frame or greenhouse over winter, keeping an eye on the soil and maintaining a moist compost.

In order for the bulbs to develop properly they need a month or two with temperatures of between 0-10C (32-50F). Planting later October to November or early spring gives the bulbs these cool temperatures so they can form.

Your garlic will come as a whole bulb. You need to carefully break it into the individual cloves before you plant it. Brush off the papery skin and gently break the bulb into cloves, avoiding causing any damage as you do. Remember that the pointy end goes upwards and the flatter end goes down, as that is where the roots come from.

Growing Garlic

Keep your garlic well-watered, particularly during dry spells as the water is necessary for the bulb's growth. Avoid getting water on leaves as this encourages fungal growth which can kill the plant.

Garlic is a low maintenance plant, just make sure you keep the weeds down in its bed as it does not appreciate competition. So long as you plant it at the right time of year for the variety you have you should get some nice garlic bulbs at harvest time. A single bulb of garlic can have anything from 12 to 20 cloves on it, which is usually plenty for even the most extreme garlic fan. Usually though, garlic is sold in packs of 2 or even 3 bulbs, meaning you will have a LOT of garlic at harvest time. Dry it and store it so you can use it later in the year and you may even end up giving some away to friends or family to use up the excess.

If you grow a particularly good crop of garlic, then you should keep a couple of cloves to one side for planting the following year. Over time you can even develop your own strain of garlic that is specifically developed for your area by keeping the best two or three bulbs each year and replanting them.

Fertilizing, Mulching & Watering

Garlic does take a long time to mature, anything from 180 to 210 days depending on the variety, which can put some people off growing it. It is important that the plant is well cared for during this time in order to produce the best possible crop.

Fertilising Garlic
As garlic is such a long season crop it is a surprisingly heavy feeder. Therefore, it is very important that you plan in advance, preparing the soil to provide all the nutrients that garlic requires. Good preparation means less work to do during the growing season!

Depending on the variety, you will plant any time from late October to February. Before planting, dig in plenty of fertiliser such as manure, blood meal or chicken manure pellets. This will give the soil a high level of nutrients which the garlic will use as it grows. It reduces the amount you need to feed your plants during their growing season.

In the spring, fertilize your garlic with a high nitrogen fertilizer such as chicken pellets. Scatter this on top of the soil and it will break down over the next few weeks, releasing its nutrients into the soil where the garlic can use it. You can carefully dig in the fertilizer, working it into the soil between rows if you prefer.

Plan to fertilize your garlic every three or four weeks in order to keep the nutrient levels high.

In early May, give your garlic another high nitrogen feed and thereafter use a feed that is lower in nitrogen as high nitrogen levels can cause bulb growth to be stunted.

From the end of June, you can stop fertilising your plants as the bulbs should be getting close to harvesting.

Watering Garlic

Garlic appreciates a good watering and will benefit from a deep watering every eight to ten days from spring to June. If the weather is wet then you do not need to water as frequently, but in extreme dry weather you may need to increase the frequency of watering.

By the end of June, stop watering as you want the bulb to dry out before harvesting it.

Water direct to the soil, avoiding getting water on the leaves. Wet leaves encourage fungal diseases which can destroy your crop. If you cannot avoid watering the leaves, then at least water first thing in the morning so that the leaves have the day to dry out. Avoid watering in the evening as the cooler nights can mean water sits on the soil or leaves, encouraging pests and diseases.

In early to mid-July you can dig up one of your garlic bulbs to check whether it is ready. You are looking for a nice plump clove that has a thick, papery, dry skin.

Mulching Garlic

Mulch your garlic bed with 6-12" of straw when you plant. This insulates the ground, which helps the garlic get established and grow a strong root system. The mulch also helps to keep weeds down, which garlic appreciates as it doesn't compete well. In spring the garlic will push through the mulch and grow normally. The mulch helps to retain moisture and keep the soil warm, which can help your garlic mature.

Garlic isn't a needy plant when it comes to looking after it. So long as you keep down the competition, regularly water and feed it you should end up with a great crop. So long as you dry and store it correctly, you will have fresh garlic for months!

Harvesting, Curing, Storing & Preserving

This is a very important chapter for anyone growing garlic because looking after your crop means that you get fresh garlic for 6 to 12 months, depending on the variety and how it is stored. There are also many other ways of preserving garlic other than just drying it out, which you will learn later in this chapter.

If you want your crop to last then you need to preserve it correctly, and drying is a very important part of this. Garlic that isn't dried correctly will start to send up green shoots as it sprouts. This growth sucks the goodness out of the cloves and you end up with a withered husk which is no good for anything.

Harvesting Garlic
Timing is vital when it comes to harvesting garlic as leaving it too long can mean one of the diseases or pests that affect garlic takes hold or that the bulb splits because it over-matures. However, being an underground crop

it is a difficult one to determine whether it is mature and ready to harvest.

Onions are easy to harvest as you wait until the foliage dies back and then harvest them as and when convenient. Garlic though, is not as forgiving and if you wait until the leaves have died right back then your bulbs will have matured too much and the cloves start to separate out from each other. Although the garlic can still be used, it will not store as long as it could.

However, harvesting too early means the bulbs haven't formed properly and also will not store as well!

Most people agree that garlic is harvested when a few of the lower leaves turn brown but a half dozen or so of the top leaves are still green. Depending on your climate, when they were planted and the weather since planting this can be anywhere from early July through to late August. Basically, from the end of June keep an eye on the leaves and even dig up a bulb to check for maturity.

Do not try to harvest garlic by pulling it up by the above ground growth. All that will happen is the leaves will snap off and it could damage the bulb.

Loosen the soil around the bulb with a fork before lifting by hand, or just lift with a fork, carefully avoiding damaging the bulb.

Once harvested, gently brush off excess dirt, but do not wash. Avoid brushing off the papery skin, which protects the garlic during storage.

The best bulbs with the biggest cloves can be stored and saved for planting the next season, which is a great way of growing more of your favorite varieties of garlic.

Curing Garlic
This is the process of drying out garlic ready for storage. Once the garlic is lifted you will trim the roots before curing. Softneck varieties can be dried with the foliage on, which is often braided to allow for easy storage. If it is not being braided, then cut the stalks off once the garlic is cured. Hardneck varieties have the foliage cut to within an inch or two of the bulb once it is dry.

Garlic, unlike onions, needs to be cured out of direct sunlight. Move the garlic to somewhere dry, out of direct sunlight, such as a garage, and allow them to dry. Wherever you put them requires good air circulation to allow the garlic to dry fully.

It can take anything from a couple of weeks to a couple of months for garlic to dry fully, depending on the weather at the time. In damper or more humid weather, the drying process will take much longer than it hot, dry weather. Don't be tempted to move them into full sun as that will damage the bulbs.

Storing Garlic
Fresh garlic can be stored in a cool, dry, dark place where it will last anything up to a year, depending on the variety and the conditions. Make sure wherever you store it is out of direct sunshine as that will reduce the storage time significantly.

You can buy special garlic keepers which allow for good air circulation, though the traditional way is to braid the garlic (softneck varieties only) and hang it. This allows for air to circulate properly and the garlic will keep well.

Garlic should never be stored in a refrigerator as even at those cooler temperatures, harmful bacteria will start to form in about a week. Amongst other things the bacteria that causes botulism can form, which can be fatal to humans.

Just hanging the garlic somewhere cool and dark with good air flow is sufficient for storing your garlic. Alternatively, you can peel the cloves and freeze them. Some people will mince the fresh garlic, put it in ice cube trays and fill them with water. When you need to add garlic to a dish you just get an ice cube and throw it in the pan; the water melts and the garlic cooks as normal. You don't need to defrost the garlic before using it whether you freeze it whole or minced. If you are freezing your garlic, then you should freeze it immediately after preparing it, rather than storing it in your refrigerator or at room temperature for any length of time.

You can store garlic in oil, but you need to be very careful that it doesn't develop bacteria. Usually a preservative such as citric acid is added to the oil to prevent bacteria from growing in water droplets that get trapped in the oil. As garlic is a low acid food it is prone to bacteria formation.

Garlic has the mildest taste when it is harvested and cured. Once it starts to dry the garlic bulb loses mass, which makes the pungency or garlic flavor increase, so the taste gets stronger. If you want to maintain the mild garlic flavor then you need to slice and dehydrate the garlic after curing.

You should also remember that the growing conditions from the soil to the climate can influence the taste and strength of the garlic cloves.

Pickling is an option to store garlic as the vinegar acts as a preservative and will destroy any harmful bacteria. One benefit of pickled garlic is you don't end up with garlic breath because the acidic vinegar neutralises the compound responsible for that effect. Pickled garlic does retain many of its health benefits. Pickled it can be stored for as much as 5 or 6 years!

Pickling Garlic

There are a number of different ways to pickle garlic, depending on your preference and tastes. You can use anything from malt vinegar to the more exotic white or red wine vinegar for preserving your garlic.

Pickling in Malt Vinegar

Malt vinegar (brown vinegar) is very easy to get hold of and cheap. It is great for pickling most things from onions to eggs to gherkins. You can pickle your garlic in it too with this simple recipe. Feel free to adjust the spices depending on availability and your personal preferences.

Ingredients
- 10oz (300g) garlic cloves
- 1¾oz (50g) white sugar
- 1¼ cups (300ml) malt vinegar
- 1 teaspoon fennel seeds
- 12 pink peppercorns
- 3 whole, dry bay leaves
- Pinch of saffron

Method
1. Break up the bulb into individual cloves and place in a large bowl
2. Pour boiling water over the garlic until it is covered
3. Leave for 20-30 seconds and then drain
4. Return the garlic to the bowl and cover in cold water
5. Peel the garlic, the skins should be easy to remove now
6. Put the vinegar into a saucepan together with the saffron and sugar and bring to the boil
7. Simmer for 2 minutes
8. Put the peeled garlic into a sterilised jar (Kilner jars work well) together with the peppercorns, bay leaves and fennel
9. Fill the jar with vinegar until the garlic is covered

10. Seal and leave for 7-10 days, shaking occasionally, before eating

Pickling with Red/White Wine Vinegar

For a bit more flavor you can use a red or white wine vinegar as the base for your pickling. This gives the garlic a much more rounded and intense, though not garlicky, flavor. Again, feel free to adjust the spices to your personal tastes.

Ingredients
- 3 whole garlic cloves
- 1¼ pints (700ml) white wine vinegar, red wine vinegar or apple cider vinegar
- 1 whole dried chilli or ½ teaspoon dried chilli flakes
- 1 teaspoon whole mustard seeds
- 1 teaspoon pure salt (table salt will make the mixture cloudy)
- 3 whole all spice berries
- Sprig of fresh basil

Method
1. Break the garlic bulbs into cloves, discarding excess papery skin
2. Sterilize a preserving jar
3. Blanch the garlic for 60 seconds in boiling water and then cool rapidly to loosen the skins for easy peeling
4. Put all the spices into your sterilized jar
5. Add the garlic cloves
6. Bring the vinegar to the boil, simmer for 1-2 minutes
7. Pour into the sterilized jar
8. Seal and allow to cool for 12-24 hours before refrigerating

How to Braid Garlic

A popular way to store garlic is by braiding it and hanging it. Many people still use this traditional method. A more modern alternative is to use lady's pantyhose (tights). You cut the pair in half at the crotch, then put a garlic bulb in to one leg, tying a knot about it, then adding another, tying a knot above it and so on until the leg is full. You then simple cut the material below the bottom knot to access the garlic as you need it. I find this way the easiest way to store garlic or onions, but braiding is a very traditional method and looks fantastic hanging in your garage or shed.

For a single braid, you will need 13 garlic bulbs. Cut the roots to one inch long and carefully brush off any soil from the bulbs. Leave the stalks on the bulb, though remove any wilted or diseased leaves.

Select the three biggest bulbs to start your braid with. Lay them out on a table with on bulb at the top and then the two others slightly below it on either side.

Take the leaves from the left-hand bulb and fold them over the necks of the other two bulbs, then wrap them underneath. Pull the leaves tight which secures the bottom three bulbs together.

Take the next bulb and put it on top and in the middle of these three onions, lining the leaves up with those of the middle onion. You'll see three strands of leaves which need braiding together twice, just like hair, and making sure it is tight.

Add another two garlic bulbs, one on either side of the braid, lining their leaves up with the outside bulbs. Braid the leaves together twice.

Continue adding one bulb to the middle, braiding twice, adding two onions, braiding twice until you have used up all 13 garlic bulbs. The top of the garlic braid finishes with just one bulb.

The top of the braid is then tied securely using garden twine or sisal. Wrap the twine around the top of the braid, pull tight and then tie off.

The braid is then hung in an appropriate place and left to dry.

Depending on the variety and the storage conditions, your garlic can last anything up to a year. You need to keep an eye on it and if it shows any signs of going off then you should either use it or discard it. With its longevity, you can enjoy home grown garlic for most of the year.

Diseases & Pests

Although garlic is quite a hardy plant, it does suffer from some pests and diseases, many of which also afflict onions and leeks. Poor weather, too much rain, fluctuating temperatures and more can encourage pests and diseases, but knowing what you are looking for will help reduce the damage to your crop.

If the temperature fluctuates too much in the spring then you can find your plants produce garlic cloves in the stem, above the ground. These, known as top sets, happen and there is nothing you can do about it except use them as normal!

Hardneck garlic varieties will produce flower stalks, which you cannot prevent. As soon as you spot these flower stalks, remove them and either use them in a salad or stir fry. You are less likely to see flower stalks in softneck varieties unless the temperatures have been too high or there hasn't been enough rain.

Later in the growing season, you can see bulbs splitting, which means you are harvesting them too late. If you harvest too late and do not plant deep enough then you can find cloves turning green. These green cloves can be used as normal, but they do not store very well.

Many pests and diseases build up in the soil, so it is important that you rotate your garlic into different areas of your garden on a 3 or 4-year cycle. What this means is that you plant garlic in an area and then do not plant garlic or any other member of the allium family (leeks, onions, etc.) in the same area for 3 or 4 years. This will help to prevent harmful pests and diseases building up in your soil.

One of the main way diseases are introduced into a crop is through using diseased seeds. Certified garlic bulbs are best for planting because you know they are disease free. Although you can plant garlic bought from the supermarket, you have no idea of whether it is carrying a potentially harmful disease which could destroy your crop.

If your plants are afflicted with a disease then remove all infected plant material and destroy it, burning is best. Whatever you do, do not compost it as the disease can probably survive the composting process and will then be spread all over your garden when you use it.

Common Diseases

These are some of the most common diseases you will encounter when growing garlic. Regular inspection of your crop will help to reduce the impact of these.

Rust (Puccinia Porri)

This is an airborne, fungal disease that thrives in dry conditions and high humidity. Planting your garlic too close together will encourage the spread of rust, so ensure you follow the spacing guidelines so there is sufficient air flow around the plants.

This disease is noticeable by small yellow or white spots starting on the leaves which turn into reddish orange blisters. Digging in sulphate of potash from February will help reduce the risk of this disease as will spraying regularly with sulfur compounds.

If this is a common problem with your crops, then try growing a spring planting variety of garlic as sometimes the damp conditions over winter can trigger the development of rust.

White Rot (Sclerotium Cepivorum)
Another fungal disease, but this time soil borne which affects all members of the allium family, most notably, onions.

The early symptoms of this disease are a fluffy, white growth underground following by the leaves dying off.

Unfortunately, this is a very difficult disease to fight and it can take decades for the fungus to die off in the soil naturally. If you discover this them immediately remove all the plants and destroy them. Also, remove the soil and dispose of it to try to avoid leaving any spores behind.

Bulb Mites
These are a member of the arachnid family and are noticeable by stunted growth and the bulbs rotting in the ground. The pest itself is a very small, creamy white colored mite with a bulbous body. When this mite damages a garlic crop it makes the bulb vulnerable to secondary infection with other diseases which can then kill off the crop completely.

This can be avoided by good crop rotation to prevent the mite building up in the soil. Treating the seed bulbs with hot water can help reduce mite populations if it has been a problem and you are reusing your own bulbs. If you are buying certified bulbs, then they will be free of this mite.

Downy Mildew
This is a fuzzy, grey / purple growth that is found on the leaf surface. Initially, you may spot pale spots or even long discolored patches on the leaves. As the disease progresses, the leaves grow paler until they yellow and the tips of the leaves collapse.

This disease is most common when the leaves are wet, often from watering from above rather than at the base, and during cooler summers.

Working a 3 or 4-year rotation system will help to minimize the risk of this disease. Using certified bulbs will ensure you do not introduce the disease into your garden. Well-draining soil and good crop spacing will also help to reduce the risk of downy mildew.

Should you find this on your garlic plants, all infected plants must be destroyed; do not compost them. There are foliar fungicides you can use to fight downy mildew; apply according to manufacturer's instructions, ensuring the leaves are thoroughly coated.

Leaf Miners

These insects will leave very thin, winding, white colored trails on the leaves of your garlic plants. In heavy infestations, the leaves will have large white blotches on them and drop from the plant. Infected plants will have smaller, less well developed bulbs.

The adult leaf minter is a small fly, black and yellow in color, that lays eggs on the leaves. These hatch and the larvae then feed on the inside of the leaves. When the larvae mature, they drop off the leaves on to the soil where they pupate. In warm weather, the life cycle of the leaf miner can be as short as two weeks, so in a single growing year there can easily be seven to ten generations of this pest.

Removing your garlic as soon as it is ready will help reduce the risk of this pest. If you are transplanting garlic grown elsewhere, check it carefully for leaf miners before planting. Avoid using insecticides on your garlic crop unless you have spotted this pest, as excess spraying will kill off the natural predators of the leaf miner.

Lesion Nematode

Symptoms of this pest are stunted growth, a lack of fine roots in the root system and lesions growing on the roots. This particular pest isn't too fussy about what it infests and will happily attack garlic as well as a wide variety of other crops.

Because these nematodes attack such a wide variety of plants, crop rotation isn't a particularly effective control. Most commonly hot water dips are used to control these nematodes, though using certified bulbs will reduce the risk of introducing these pests into your growing beds.

Garlic Mosaic Virus

When infected, you will see mosaic like patterns on the leaves or streaks plus stunted growth and reduced yields. This disease is transmitted by aphids and a plant can be infected without having any symptoms. You will often find this disease together with another viral infection.

Infected plants need to be destroyed, not composted. The best way to avoid this is to plant certified, virus free cloves.

Onion Maggot

Another pest that causes stunted growth or wilting plants. This maggot usually infects your plants when the bulbs are forming and will cause deformed bulbs that rot in storage.

The adult insect is a grey colored fly that lays elongated eggs at the base of the plant. Tiny, white larvae hatch and bore into the garlic plant. A mature larva is about ½" long. Female maggots live for between two and four weeks, laying several hundred eggs during their lives. The pupae bury into the soil and will survive all but the coldest winter.

Good sanitation will help here, as will crop rotation. Promptly removing garlic bulbs at the end of the growing season will deprive the maggots of their food source, so they die. Any damaged bulbs should be stored away from the rest and used first.

Any infected plants should be removed and destroyed. There are sprays that can be used but they tend to be very strong and will kill beneficial insects too. Floating row covers can stop females from laying their eggs near your garlic plants.

Purple Blotch
This disease starts off with small lesions on the stalk which grow, turning a brown to purple color, become red to purple to the outside, surrounded by a yellow area. In severe infections, the lesions will join together and even kill off the leaves.

This disease is most common when the leaves are wet and the nights have high humidity (when the disease spores). Good crop spacing and watering at the base of the plant will help to reduce the risk of infection. Good crop rotation will help as will planting in a soil that drains well. There are fungicides available to treat this disease.

Thrips
There are a number of different thrips that infect garlic, though they have similar symptoms and treatments. The leaves will be discolored, distorted and scarred. In severe infestations, the plants take on a silvery sheen.

The insects are only about 1.5mm long, with adults being anywhere from a pale yellow color through to light brown. The young (nymphs) are smaller and a lighter color.

As these thrips infect such a wide variety of plants they can be introduced from other plants you are growing. Thrips do have some natural enemies, including lacewings, pirate bugs and some predatory mites.

If there are grain crops growing near your garden then you should avoid planting garlic anywhere near to them as thrips build up on grain in the spring before looking for other hosts, such as your garlic.

If you spot an infection, then you can use an approved insecticide to kill these pests.

White Rot
This fungal infection is often spotted by the older leaves turning yellow. Growth is then stunted; the leaves die and you will see a fluffy white growth on the bulb which can spread to the leaves.

Unfortunately, this disease is very hard to get rid of, and if it gets established then you cannot use that area to grow any member of the allium family for at least 20 years. The fungus can remain dormant in the soil for up to 20 years and is considered one of the most devastating diseases that affect garlic.

Providing weather conditions are not favorable to this disease (i.e. Damp and humid), you can use a fungicide to treat white rot. By not transferring soil between sites you can prevent the spread of this fungus and certified bulbs will be disease free. A 3 or 4-year crop rotation cycle will prevent the build-up of this fungus in your soil.

Eel Worm
This is a fairly common soil born pest and is often referred to as "stem and bulb eel worm" because of the areas it attacks. Weeds support eel worms, so keeping your garlic patch weed free will help to keep the population down. Hot water treatments can be used on bulbs that are going to be stored. There are no chemical treatments available for the home grower against eel worm. Some people apply Jeyes Fluid to the soil before planting as this will kill eel worms.

Companion Planting

Companion planting is a natural way of keeping pests and diseases at bay by putting plants that complement each other next to each other. Although old time gardeners have been using this for years, younger gardeners are discovering these techniques and benefiting from these natural controls.

For example, vineyards will often be surrounded by rose bushes. They aren't there just to look pretty, but to act as an early warning system! Should aphids come into the area they will attack the roses before moving on to the valuable grape vines. Therefore, the farmers inspect the roses and take action when they notice the aphids before the infestation damages their crops.

Companion planting is a huge subject as there are so many plants that work well together, e.g. Tomato and basil plants being grown together. We'll focus in this section on garlic and its uses as a companion plant.

Although garlic does suffer from pests itself, it is naturally a repellent for a wide variety of pests and even fungal diseases! Some gardeners will grow garlic scattered over the garden as a companion plant. In these cases, because you are only growing a few cloves, crop rotation becomes less important, but as you rotate the main crops, you tend to also rotate the companion plant too.

As garlic takes up so little space and has so many uses, it is very popular as a companion crop, being relatively easy to grow and tolerant of a wide variety of soil conditions.

Garlic can help drive away a wide variety of pests, including:

- Ants
- Aphids
- Cabbage Loopers
- Codling Moths
- Fungus Gnats
- Japanese Beetles
- Onion Flies
- Snails
- Spider Mites

Garlic has even proven a deterrent for rabbit and deer, which can be extremely destructive to your crops.

For best results as a companion plant it should be planted in November time, so that it builds up plenty of sulfur and is above the ground when you are planting its companions. Of course, if you miss this planting window, you can get it planted in January or February, but you need to make sure it is established. Later plantings can benefit from a top dressing of sulfur in order for the garlic to be pungent enough to do its job.

Garlic grows well with a huge number of plants, helping to protect them from pests and diseases. Perhaps my favorite is to plant garlic or onions next to carrots as the smell confuses the carrot fly so it cannot destroy your carrot crop!

Other good companions for garlic include:

- Beets
- Broccoli
- Cabbage
- Cauliflower
- Dill
- Eggplant
- Fruit Trees
- Geraniums
- Kale
- Kohlrabi
- Marigolds

- Nasturtiums
- Peppers
- Potatoes
- Roses
- Spinach
- Tomatoes

As well as garlic being beneficial to other plants, there are some plants that you can plant near garlic which help make the garlic better. Rue is often planted to drive off maggots, whilst chamomile will improve the flavor of the garlic. Yarrow and summer savory are other plants which are known to help protect garlic from pests and diseases.

However, not all plants will appreciate garlic being planted near to it, and some will suffer when planted in the vicinity of garlic, particularly with stunted growth. Asparagus, beans, parsley, peas and sage should all be planted well away from garlic to prevent any problems with growth.

Companion planting is an excellent way for you to reduce your reliance on chemicals and is ideal for the organic gardener. It is extremely effective and has been used for hundreds if not thousands of years to help strengthen plants and produce good crops.

All you need to do is plant cloves near the crops that need the companion and allow it to grow. At the end of the growing season you have a great crop of garlic (don't leave it to go over-ripe) and a healthy crop of its companion too!

Therapeutic Uses of Garlic

Garlic has been used in medicine for thousands of years and is still a popular folk remedy, used for everything and anything! Modern scientific research is studying garlic very closely because scientists have realized that this plant is incredibly beneficial to the human body when used correctly.

There are so many conditions treated with garlic, including high and low blood pressure (it acts to equalize your blood pressure), high cholesterol, coronary heart disease, hardened arteries, a wide variety of cancers including prostrate, yeast infections and much more.

Obviously, you should not self-prescribe garlic for anything without consulting your doctor first. This chapter will detail some of the folk remedies as well as show you how garlic is being used as a medicine to combat a wide variety of modern ailments.

There are literally pages and pages of potential uses for garlic, it being an antibiotic and an antifungal, making it great at treating yeast infections, jock itch and athlete's foot. The only downside of garlic appears to be the fact that it leaves you with stinky breath and pores, you can sweat garlic if you consume too much of it.

Some people do suffer from an allergy to garlic to varying degrees. If you are allergic to garlic in any way you should never use it unless you are under medical supervision. If you are unsure if you are allergic to garlic but suffer from other allergies you should get tested by a professional prior to taking any garlic. Some people can be allergic to fresh garlic but not dried or powder, whereas other people are allergic to garlic in any form.

Garlic is most commonly self-prescribed as raw garlic; cooking it does destroy several the beneficial enzymes, but it can still have a positive effect even when cooked. Medicinally, garlic usually has the active ingredients extracted and inserted into a cream or a pill, though you can get garlic powder pills (they'll still make you smell though).

Antifungal Properties of Garlic

One of the most popular uses of garlic is as an anti-fungal agent, something that has been proven in many scientific research programs. The anti-fungal properties are down to allicin, which is a phytochemical produced when you chop or crush raw garlic cloves. To maximize allicin levels, leave the crushed or chopped garlic to sit for 10 to 15 minutes before using it, either raw or cooked. Allicin is a very strong antioxidant, which is extremely beneficial to you plus it is high in vitamin C, selenium and zinc, all of which are essential to your health.

These antioxidants help to protect your body from the harmful effects of free radicals, which cause cellular damage, including the signs of ageing, by attacking healthy cells. Free radicals are known to contribute to a variety of conditions including diabetes, heart problems, rheumatoid arthritis, dementia and some types of cancer.

The best known benefit of antioxidants is that they reduce premature ageing of the skin because of its ability to neutralize free radicals.

Garlic is used to treat acne and yeast infections because it is a powerful anti-fungal agent. Some people believe it is beneficial for dandruff sufferers as that is often caused by a fungal infection, but little research has been performed on this.

Powerful Natural Antibiotic

In the 1800s, Louis Pasteur, the discoverer of penicillin, found garlic to be a powerful antibacterial agent. It killed bacteria just like penicillin did and was widely used during the First and Second World Wars for its antibacterial properties, being popular because of its easy availability. With supply lines under pressure it was often difficult to transport penicillin to where it was needed, but garlic was easy to obtain and kept well.

More recent medical studies have confirmed that garlic is not only effective against bacteria but also has strong antiviral properties. It fights and heals infections that have been caused by worms and other microbes too.

In modern medicine garlic is often used to fight bacteria which has developed resistance to common antibiotic drugs. This use is still being researched, but initial results are promising and should result in highly effective antibacterial treatments.

Anti-Cancer Effects
This is possibly one of the most exciting uses for garlic and research is underway across the world to use garlic to fight cancer. Raw garlic, more so than cooked garlic, and garlic extracts have strong anti-cancer effects, particularly against colon and stomach cancer.

These anti-cancer effects seem to come from a number of different mechanisms, including the antioxidant properties to inhibit free radicals. Garlic also activates enzymes which detoxify carcinogens and it regulates the cell-cycle arrest. As well as this, garlic induces apoptosis which is a natural process of killing unwanted or abnormal cells. Cancer cells typically avoid this process, but garlic can cause the cells to die.

Garlic Helps People with Insulin Resistance
A diet rich in garlic also helps people who suffer from insulin resistance, which is linked to a number of diseases, including type 2 diabetes, pre-diabetes, adult acne, heart disease and excess body fat, particularly around the waistline. It helps the body's cells respond properly to insulin.

It is believed that this benefit comes from the garlic oil and a compound called dialysis trisulfide which is found in garlic. Both of these appear to improve the way the body responds to insulin and so decreases insulin resistance.

Benefits for Psoriasis
Eating garlic is beneficial for anyone who suffers from psoriasis as garlic inhibits the activity of an enzyme known as lipoxygenase. Psoriasis sufferers typically have high levels of arachidonic acid in their adipose skin and tissues. The lipoxygenase enzyme helps to reduce the inflammation caused by this acid.

Raw garlic, ounce for ounce, has five times the vitamin C found in carrots plus is high in both selenium and zinc. These all contribute to the antioxidant properties of garlic, which reduces oxidative stress, a cause of skin inflammation, in psoriasis patients.

If using garlic for your psoriasis, you should crush or chop it and leave it for 10-15 minutes to maximize the amount of allicin and other beneficial nutrients. Be aware of the potential side effects of suddenly increasing your garlic intake such as your sweat smelling of garlic, your breath smelling of garlic, a mild upset stomach, heartburn and sometimes dizziness.

Be aware that if you have stomach ulcers, any bleeding disorder or you are on anti-coagulant or anti-platelet medications then you must refrain from using garlic until you have consulted with your doctor. Likewise, if you are pregnant, breast feeding or awaiting surgery, then you should also speak to your doctor to ensure the garlic isn't going to cause any problems.

Garlic and Acne

The properties of garlic make it extremely helpful in treating acne. In Ayurvedic medicine (traditional Indian medicine), raw garlic is considered the best natural remedy for adult acne. It is also considered beneficial to reducing acne scars and preventing further acne developing. There are also reports that eating raw garlic prevents and gets rid of spots and pimples. However, you do have to get past the smell of having eaten garlic for these beauty benefits.

Garlic contains high levels of vitamins and phytonutrients which are known to battle acne. Zinc is vital for controlling sebum, which is a major contributor to acne. As garlic also combats insulin resistance, it can also help prevent adult acne. Insulin resistance is linked to acne and obviously can lead to diabetes.

Although you will suffer from the usual side effects of eating garlic, it isn't necessarily the most social of plants. However, people who have acne rosacea need to be careful. In studies, around 11% of people who have this condition listed garlic as a trigger food and it made their rosacea worse.

Be aware that garlic does have blood thinning properties which is why you need to be careful of taking it if this will have a negative effect on you. If you are on any medication you should check with your pharmacist to ensure it is safe to use garlic as it can prevent certain medications from working.

Garlic and the Common Cold

As you have already learnt, garlic has a wide range of beneficial properties, which leads to it being believed to help combat the flu and the common cold. Several studies have taken place to determine whether this is true.

This research has shown that eating garlic can help to prevent cold, so people who eat garlic suffer from fewer colds, but garlic does not provide a cure for the common cold. The research has indicated that eating garlic may slightly reduce the amount of time you have a cold.

The active components of garlic plus its high levels of zinc and vitamin are proven to reduce the symptoms of a cold and provide some protection against infection. The allicin in the garlic helps to protect you from cold and flu viruses (remember that garlic has strong antiviral properties).

As with taking garlic for any condition, you need to be aware of the limitations and probably side effects of it. However, it can help fight infection and keep you healthy.

Medicinal Uses of Garlic

As you already know, garlic has been used traditionally to treat a wide variety of complaints. Medical researchers are very excited about the properties of garlic and are working to determine how to use it effectively. In this section, you will learn about some of this medical research, much of which is still underway. You will find out what medical researchers consider garlic to be possibly effective in treating, what it is ineffective in treating and what areas they consider need further research before a conclusion can be drawn.

Possibly Effective in Treating

Research has shown that garlic is possible effective in treating these conditions:

- Atherosclerosis (hardening of the arteries) – garlic helps to maintain the flexibility of arteries and stop them hardening. Research has indicated that a garlic powder supplement taken twice daily for 24 months reduces hardening of the arteries. Over a four-year period, research has shown that women receive more benefits than men.
- Colon / Rectal Cancer – research has shown that eating garlic reduces the risk of developing both rectal or colon cancer. Taking high doses of an aged garlic extract every day for a year does reduce the risk of developing new tumors in people with certain types of these cancers.
- High Blood Pressure – sufferers of high blood pressure benefit from an oral garlic powder supplement. Research has indicated that a reduction in blood pressure of around 7-8%.
- Prostate Cancer – in China, men who consume a clove of garlic

every day appear to have half the chance of developing prostate cancer. Research in areas where lots of garlic is eaten has shown that it does reduce the risk of this type of cancer. Research is still not decided on how effective garlic is against prostate cancer, but early results from a clinical study indicate that garlic extract supplements both reduces the risk and reduces symptoms.

- Tick Bites – although there is no research comparing garlic to commercial tick repellents, people who eat a lot of garlic over a two-month period are less likely to be bitten by tick.
- Ringworm – using a gel that contains 0.6% ajoene (one of the chemical components of garlic), twice daily for seven days is as effective as an anti-fungal medication in the treatment of ringworm.
- Jock Itch – the same gel as used for ringworm is just as effective as anti-fungal medication.
- Athlete's Foot – using a gel with 1% ajoene is as effective as the often prescribed Lamisil in treating athlete's foot.

Possibility Ineffective in Treating

Research has taken place into using garlic to treat these conditions but at present it does not have a significant effect in treating these conditions.

- Breast Cancer – there is no evidence that eating garlic reduces the risk of developing breast cancer.
- Cystic Fibrosis – research indicates garlic is of no active benefit to anyone suffering this condition.
- Diabetes – although garlic helps to manage insulin resistance, garlic does not appear to have any effect on blood sugar levels.
- High Cholesterol – research is inconsistent here, with some indicating garlic is beneficial to high cholesterol suffers and it certainly doesn't seem to have any effect after six months of use.
- Lung Cancer – there is no indication that garlic reduces the risk of lung cancer.
- Mosquito Repellent – although traditionally thought to repel mosquitos due to you "sweating" garlic, research does not substantiate this claim.

Insufficient Current Evidence

The following conditions are being researched and at present there is not enough evidence to show that garlic is beneficial.

- Hair Loss – a gel with 5% garlic used topically with a steroid does

increase hair growth when used for three months.
- Angina – research indicates that intravenous garlic administered for ten days does reduce chest pain when compared to the traditional treatment of nitroglycerin.
- Common Cold – as discussed early, garlic appears to help reduce the duration and frequency of colds, though not significantly.
- Corns – garlic extract, particularly one that dissolves in fat, applied twice daily improves corns after 10 to 20 days of use.
- Esophagus Cancer – early research is inconsistent with some studies showing raw garlic to reduce the risk whereas others showing it does not.
- Muscle Aches – taking allicin every day for 14 days appears to reduce muscle soreness after exercise.
- Exercise Performance – a 900mg dose of garlic prior to exercise appears to improve endurance, particularly among young athletes.
- Hepatitis – garlic oil and diphenyl-dimethyl-dicarboxylate taken together improves liver function in hepatitis sufferers. Research is not clear on the effect of garlic by itself.
- Lead Poisoning – garlic taken three times a day for a month can reduce lead levels in the blood of people who have lead poisoning. However, so far it doesn't appear to be any more effective than the usual medication.
- Thrush – garlic paste applied around the mouth helps speed up the healing time for people with oral thrush.
- Mouth Ulcers – a garlic mouthwash used three times a day for a month does help people with mouth ulcers, but it isn't as effective as drugs like nystatin. Despite the side effects of garlic (smell) people in the research were more satisfied with the garlic mouthwash rather than the medicinal one.
- Warts – applying a fat-soluble garlic extract to hand warts twice a day does remove then in a couple of weeks. A water-soluble garlic extract is less effective and takes as many as 30 to 40 days to be effective.

Side Effects & Safety Advice

As a natural product, garlic is surprisingly safe to take. However, there are some people who suffer from an allergy to garlic and depending on the severity of the allergy, they should avoid or be very careful taking garlic.

Most commonly, garlic is taken by mouth and this can cause bad breath, bad body odor, heartburn, gas, vomiting, and upset stomach or even a burning sensation in the mouth or stomach.

Garlic does increase the risk of bleeding so if you have had surgery or are scheduled for surgery, you should avoid garlic. Some people who have taken garlic have reported their asthma symptoms have deteriorated, so should you suffer from asthma, monitor your condition if you choose to take garlic.

Most people will be okay applying garlic topically. Some people experience skin damage like a burn when applying garlic to their skin. Raw garlic can cause intense irritation when applied directly to the skin. If you are using a garlic gel, paste or mouthwash, then it should not be used for longer than three months.

Garlic is typically safe to use during pregnancy if consumed as part of a normal diet. Taking medicinal amounts during both pregnancy and breast-feeding is potentially unsafe and should not be taken without medical supervision. Avoid applying any garlic products to the skin during pregnancy or breast-feeding as there is not currently enough information to determine its safety.

Garlic is safe for children to eat as part of their normal diet, but care needs to be taken when providing any oral supplements. Short term it is likely safe, but high doses can be dangerous and potentially fatal to children. The evidence for this is sketchy, but a warning has been issued so better safe than sorry. Garlic applied topically can burn children's skin.

Garlic should be avoided by anyone with any type of bleeding disorder as it can increase the risk of bleeding. Stop taking garlic supplements at least two weeks before any surgery and do not resume taking it until given the all clear by your physician. Likewise, anyone with stomach or digestion problems should avoid garlic because it can irritate your stomach and intestines.

As garlic works to lower blood pressure, anyone with low blood pressure should avoid taking any garlic supplements. It could, in theory, drop your blood pressure down to dangerous levels.

Interactions with Other Drugs
Many natural remedies can interact adversely with medication. Therefore, if you are on any type of medication, you should consult with your doctor before taking any garlic for therapeutic purposes.

The following drugs are known to interact with garlic and if you are taking any of these then you should avoid any garlic except that in a normal diet.

- Isoniazid (Nydrazid, INH) – garlic can reduce the quantity of this drug your body absorbs and the effectiveness of it.
- HIV/AIDS Medication – Non-Nucleoside Reverse Transcriptase Inhibitors (NNRTIs) also interact negatively with garlic. Garlic will increase the speed the body breaks down this medication and can, therefore, reduce the effectiveness of the medication.
- Saquinavir or Fortovase or Invirase – garlic can increase the speed the body breaks down these drugs and could decrease their effectiveness.

The following drugs are known to interact with garlic at a moderate level, meaning you should be cautious if you are on any of these drugs and seek medical advice to dosage / usage,

- Birth Control Pills – garlic can increase the speed with which the body breaks down the estrogen found in contraceptive pills. It can decrease the effectiveness of the birth control. If you are taking garlic, then you should use an additional method of birth control.
- Cyclosporine – garlic can increase the speed with which the body breaks this drug down.
- Medications Changed by the Liver – certain medications are broken down by the liver after you take them, including acetaminophen, theophylline, and others used for anesthesia during surgery. If you are taking any garlic supplement, including garlic oil, consult with your doctor or surgeon if any medication you are taking is broken down by your liver.
- Blood Clotting Medication – any anticoagulant or anti-platelet drugs will interact with garlic, as garlic can slow blood clotting. This includes a wide variety of drugs such as warfarin, any drug containing ibuprofen (including Advil), aspirin, and many more. If you are taking any type of medication that affects your blood clotting, then you need to consult with your physician before taking garlic.
- Warfarin – this is prescribed fairly often and garlic can increase the effectiveness of this drug. If you are taking garlic together with warfarin you can find the chances of bruising and bleeding increase so will need your blood checking regularly and the warfarin dosage adjusted appropriately.

Garlic is a popular health food supplement, with many people taking garlic capsules or oil regularly. Although it is beneficial in many cases, in some situations it can be unsafe to take and can make certain conditions worse.

If you are on any medication or have any doubt about whether garlic as a supplement is harmful to you, consult with a doctor. In almost every case, normal garlic use in food will give you some of garlic's benefits, though do consult your doctor if you are taking any of the drugs discussed above.

Growing Garlic for Profit

Most people will grow garlic purely for fun and to enjoy fresh garlic throughout the year. However, some people may want to turn their hobby into a money making business. This isn't for everyone, but garlic can be turned into a profitable enterprise if you so desire.

Before you start rubbing your hands together with glee, you do have to realize that garlic isn't going to be an instant cash crop. It will take some months for it to be ready to harvest and you will have to do some work in the meantime. With patience, though, you can very easily turn a profit from this ancient crop.

There are a lot of potentially profitable crops out there such as saffron, to give but one example, but garlic is a particular favorite because it is relatively easy to grow and forgiving of soil conditions. It is the second most used spice in the whole world, trailing just behind pepper and in the USA over 300 million pounds of garlic is consumed every year!

The key to making money with garlic is to grow the varieties that people want to buy. This can be done by checking the websites of people who grow or sell garlic and see what varieties are popular. Those that sell out the fastest are going to be the most popular varieties.

Hardneck varieties such as Rocambole, Purple Stripe and Porcelain are always good sellers and often sell out very quickly. Elephant garlic is another variety that is very popular and often expensive to buy. It can be hard to get hold of as a consumer, so it can be very easy to sell because garlic fans love it and will buy lots of it when they see it.

Purple stripe garlic is one of the most popular varieties of garlic with restaurants because it has a very sweet flavor when baked. For the home cook, it is easy to peel, looks nice and stores well.

Rocambole garlic has a more savory flavor, easy to peel and makes a good garlic powder. It is considered the caviar of garlics and is very popular with chefs. It appreciates a rich soil, does well in colder climates and is easy to grow. However, it only stores for around 4 months and you must regularly remove the scrapes during the growing season.

Elephant garlic can sell for around $15 or so a pound, and a square foot of ground space will produce approximately half a pound of garlic. To the end consumer, you can often sell a single bulb for as much as $8 to $10, depending on your location and market. Using this you can calculate roughly how many square feet of space you need. So, to make $10,000 you will need about 1,250 square feet of growing space.

So firstly, you should identify the varieties you want to grow, and it can be worth growing several different varieties which can make it easier to sell what you have grown. Once you start to establish contacts within the industry, you can grow to order and even take deposits on future crop deliveries.

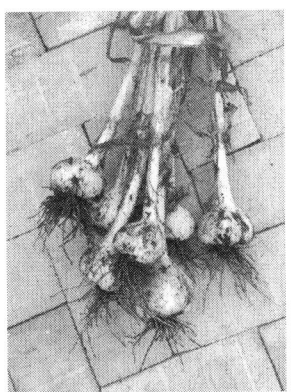

Next you need to determine where you are going to sell your garlic. Good places to sell include farmers' markets, produce brokers (they buy in bulk and resell on), local restaurants (particularly high class, French and Italian restaurants – chains are unlikely to buy from a local supplier), local supermarkets, food co-ops, stands on the side of the road and through friends and family.

This is the bit many people struggle with, but approaching your targeted outlets with samples can help you prove the quality of your product and make sales or even take orders for future delivery.

Of course, you need to ensure the garlic grows, which means careful tending of the crop and looking after it. There are insurance policies you can take out which protect you in case of crop failure. These are worth investigating, particularly if you have taken advance orders to protect your investment. For smaller crops without advance orders, this insurance is probably not financially viable.

To maximize your yield, you need to ensure your garlic growing area contains the best possible soil for growing garlic. You need a good quality soil that drains well; too much water will reduce yields. Raised beds are probably the best way to get the right soil and I've found beds that are six inches tall and a foot wide are ideal for growing garlic and maximizing the amount of garlic planted per square foot. Aim for the soil to have a pH of between 6.2 and 6.8, which garlic will appreciate.

One selling point which can justify higher prices is to grow organic garlic, but you need to be aware of what criteria you need to meet to label your produce as organic. This can be quite complex and if you incorrectly label your produce as organic you can end up in legal trouble and being fined.

When growing commercially, fertilizer is very important for healthy plants – you want one that is high in phosphorus and low in nitrogen so a strong root system develops. Prior to planting you need to use a high nitrogen fertilizer at a rate of 40 to 60 pounds per acre and then in spring add another 20 pounds per acre to ensure plenty of healthy growth.

When selling your garlic, you are best planting it about six weeks before the ground freezes. Plant too early and you will encourage disease and pest problems. The winter frosts will help ensure your garlic grows to a good size and delivers a high yield. Plant your cloves between 4 and 6 inches apart, though in raised beds with good quality soil you can plant more densely at around three inches between cloves.

Water your garlic crop regularly and keep weeds down to a minimum. During the hotter months of May to July when the bulbs are swelling you should ensure they are watered sufficiently, though be careful not to overwater them. About 2 to 3 weeks before harvesting, stop watering your garlic so it can start to dry out.

When harvested, you will need to cure and dry your garlic as normal so that it will store after you have sold it. You can braid some bulbs to sell and sell others as single bulbs.

A good outlet, if you are serious about growing garlic, is to set up your own website and sell direct to the end user. You can sell bulbs not only for culinary use, but also for other gardeners to grow at home, which works well when you grow the more unusual and in demand varieties.

Micro farms, such as any backyard gardener, seems to be the future as larger farms are struggling to be profitable. Smaller farms can respond more quickly to changing demand, have fewer running costs and can grow specialty crops that have a high profit margin. They are able to quickly shift production to a more popular and profitable crop whereas a larger farm can find it takes a season or two to switch production, by which time the crop may not be as profitable.. You can set up your own micro farm with as little as an eighth of an acre, which a lot of people will have in their back garden.

Remember that growing vertically (garlic does not have deep roots) can work very well to increase yields. Imagine you have a raised bed at ground level, then another two feet above it, and another two feet above that. From the same square footage on the ground you can grow three times the crop! There is a lot of potential with vertical gardening (see my book on this for more info) and it allows the micro farmer to maximize yields without needed large growing areas.

Growing garlic for profit is something anyone can do. You can grow it part time whilst holding down a full-time job. You can grow it as you enjoy your retirement ... it doesn't need to be a full-time concern, but it can provide some much needed extra income.

Choosing the right varieties, setting up the ideal growing conditions and then taking your garlic to market can result in a highly profitable business. When you produce good quality garlic you will find that restaurants and other outlets will want to buy your garlic every year. Just remember to keep enough so that you can replant your crop the following year!

COOKING WITH GARLIC

Garlic is a very popular plant for cooking and is used in dishes across the world. Millions of tons of garlic are used every year in meals around all over the globe and it is the second most used spice in culinary dishes, behind pepper.

In most cases, you use the bulb, dividing it into separate cloves which are then peeled and prepared for cooking. When growing your own garlic, some varieties will put up green shoots called scrapes, which can be removed and used in cooking like green onions (spring onions). However, even the leaves can be eaten, having a milder flavor than the cloves.

Some people like to pull their garlic whilst the bulbs are still small, kind of like a scallion. This green garlic is not separated into cloves and is cooked whole, giving a dish the flavor of garlic without the spiciness associated with garlic cloves. These are commonly used in Thai, Vietnamese and Chinese cooking.

When preparing a garlic clove, you cut off the top and bottom of the clove and peel all the papery white skin off. It is then chopped, crushed or cooked whole, depending on the dish you are cooking.

The flavor of garlic will vary according to the variety you use and how you prepare it. Believe it or not, crushing and chopping impart a different flavor to the garlic. Commonly it is paired in cooking with ginger, onions and tomatoes.

Some people love to roast their garlic by cutting the top of the entire bulb off, coating it all in olive oil and then roasting them in the oven. The garlic softens and is removed from the papery skin by squeezing at the root end of the clove.

Korea make something called black garlic, which is now sold worldwide. Garlic bulbs are heated over a period of several weeks which turns them very sweet and syrupy. This is very popular in Asian cuisine.

Garlic is also commonly served up as garlic bread, where garlic butter (home-made or store bought) is spread on artisan bread, heated until crispy and served.

In the stores, you can buy garlic in a wide variety of forms. Garlic powder is popular as it is easy to add to dishes and stores very well. In powdered form, it does have a different taste and is much more concentrated. An eighth of a teaspoon is equivalent to one garlic clove in cooking. It's very easy to add too much garlic powder to a dish, not realizing just how overpowering it can be.

Lazy garlic, which is chopped garlic in oil, is also popular, allowing you to use fresh garlic without the effort of cutting it up yourself. Whole garlic cloves in oil are also available, which you can then chop and use rather than having to peel them and store fresh garlic.

Garlic oils are incredibly popular too and are often seasoned with a variety of other spices too. These oils are used to give virtually any dish a nice, garlic flavor.

Another popular way of serving garlic is to smoke it. This is very difficult to do at home, but you can buy smoked garlic which is popular in the UK and Europe. It is most commonly used to stuff poultry, in stews and in soups. The entire bulb, papery skin and all is used, as most of the smoky flavor is in the usually discarded skin.

When buying garlic from a supermarket you may be presented with one or two varieties. The more expensive garlic bulbs tend to be those that are the best for flavor. It can be difficult telling the different bulbs apart, so here's some tips to help you determine what type of garlic you are buying.

Hardneck Garlic
This tends to have a stronger flavor than the softneck varieties. You will usually find between four and twelve cloves in each bulb with a hard, woody central stalk. There is usually just a single layer of bulbs, but the

central stalk tells you that it is this type of garlic. In a supermarket, you may see garlic with a purple or rosy cast on the skin. If you do, then this is more than likely hardneck garlic and is worth buying!

Hardneck garlics have a more complex taste, often being quite spicy or hot. The popular Rocambole, Purple Stripe and Porcelain varieties are all hardneck garlics. This variety needs a longer growing season and benefits from a very cold winter in order to flower in the spring.

Softneck Garlic

This variety of garlic is the most common in a supermarket as it produces more cloves, often in more than one layer. You can find anything from eight up to twenty or thirty cloves of varying sizes in a single bulb.

Softneck garlic is a very good general purpose garlic and is good in almost any type of dish. This variety is best if you are eating garlic raw or lightly cooked. It is the best type for salad dressings where garlic is the main ingredient. Typically, it has a softer flavor than hardneck garlic, with a lot less bite and a more plant like flavor.

The majority of processed garlic, such as garlic powder and seasonings, are made from softneck varieties of garlic. Artichoke is the variety most commonly found in the supermarkets and Silverskin is usually sold in braids.

Creole Garlic

For a long time, this was thought to be a variety of softneck garlic but it is actually its own variety. Usually you will find up to twelve cloves in a bulb with the color ranging from a light pink to a purple. Usually it is the whole bulb that is colored, rather than just the papery skin.

Preferring warmer climates these are harder to find and so more expensive to buy. They are usually named after wine and the most popular varieties include Creole Red, Ajo Rojo, Burgandy and Cuban Purple.

There is some heat in this garlic variety, but the pungency varies depending on which variety you use. It is worth giving the bulbs a good sniff before you buy them to get an idea of just how strong it is. You are unlikely to see this variety in a supermarket, with it more likely found in farmer's markets and specialist shops. If you do ever see it, then it is worth buying!

Black Garlic

The origins of this type of garlic are uncertain with some people attributing it to the Ancient Egyptians, whilst other people claim to have invented it in more modern times. However, it is usually found in Korean stores, though sometimes found in Japanese stores too.

The taste of this, although definitely garlic, is rich with definite plum undertones and a dash of vinegar. Like dried fruit, it is chewy and is a good alternative to use when cooking for people who are not keen on garlic.

It is made by caramelizing the natural sugars in garlic over several weeks through a combination of heat, dehydration and fermentation. During the process, the garlic turns black in color.

It is expensive, and so doesn't tend to get used in dishes like marinades. It is more commonly used in sauces and vinaigrettes and even desserts (black garlic chocolate cake is popular).

If you like garlic, then you should find this type of garlic at least once. You must go to a specialist Korean grocery store and may be surprised by the cost of it, but it is something very special that is worth tasting.

Scrapes

These are the flowering stalk that comes up from the middle of growing hardneck garlic. It usually twists and even loops as it grows, usually forming a tear drop shaped bulb at its end. This should be removed when growing garlic so that the plant puts its energy into producing a large bulb rather than seeds. When you remove it, keep it for cooking as it is delicious!

These are great sautéed in butter or oil, with a fresh, green flavor with a hint of garlic. It isn't overpowering, making it an ideal way to give a dish a hint of garlic. They are often served in salads or steamed as a side dish. They also work well when added to pasta.

You will find these coming up on your garlic plants during late spring and early summer, though you are unlikely to find them in stores.

Elephant Garlic

This are giant bulbs that are relatively difficult to get hold of, but have a lovely, mild flavor. Also known as Buffalo garlic, this is a variety of leek rather than garlic, with its Latin name being Allium Ampeloprasum rather than the Allium Sativum which is the normal sized garlic.

It is typically used as you would use a softneck garlic variety. It works very well in sauces and vinaigrettes, and is particularly delicious when roasted!

Garlic Recipes

As you know, garlic is hugely popular in cuisine and the above information has introduced you to garlic as a culinary ingredient. Now I'd like to share with you some of my favorite garlic based dishes that you can enjoy at home!

Garlic Butter
This is a great way to use your garlic and is the base for lots of delicious recipes, including garlic bread ... which you will learn shortly.

Ingredients:
- 1 cup butter (softened)
- ½ cup grated cheese (Parmesan works well but any can be substituted)
- 1 tablespoon garlic salt
- 1 tablespoon minced garlic (home grown)
- 1 teaspoon Italian seasoning
- ½ teaspoon ground black pepper
- ¼ teaspoon ground paprika

Method:
1. Mix all the ingredients together in a small bowl, until smooth
2. Refrigerate, covered, until ready to use.

Garlic Oil
This is great to use in cooking to give your meals a nice garlic flavor.

Ingredients:
- 8 garlic cloves
- 2 cups extra-virgin olive oil

Method:
1. Using the back of a knife, crush the cloves and remove the peel
2. Put the cloves into a jar
3. Cover with the oil

Garlic Bread

I love garlic bread and this can be made with any type of bread – artisan breads are best, such as ciabatta, any Italian bread or French baguettes. This recipe is based on the latter.

Ingredients:
- 1 French baguette (half sized)
- 1 stick salted butter (at room temperature)
- 4 teaspoons minced garlic
- 2 teaspoons chopped parsley
- 1 teaspoon garlic powder
- ½ teaspoon olive oil

Method:
1. Preheat your oven to 400F
2. Cut the bread lengthwise
3. Mix together the butter, garlics, parsley and olive oil in a bowl
4. For some extra flavor, mix in a couple of tablespoons of a grated cheese of your choice
5. Spread this on to the bread … be generous with it!
6. Place the bread on a baking sheet and cook for 10-15 minutes until the bread is crisp and golden brown
7. Cut into slices and serve

Roasted Garlic

This isn't for everyone, but we have mentioned roasted garlic a few times in this book, and this is the recipe!

Ingredients:
- 1 head of garlic (elephant garlic is particularly good for roasting)
- 2 to 4 tablespoons olive oil (depending on size of garlic)
- Salt and pepper to taste

Method:
1. Preheat your oven to 425F
2. Slice the top of the garlic head and put on a piece of foil
3. Drizzle olive oil inside the garlic bulb until it fills up and runs down the side
4. Wrap it tightly in the foil and put on a baking tray.
5. Bake for around 30 to 35 minutes until it is tender and fragrant
6. Remove from the oven and allow to cool
7. Peel off the outside of bulb and carefully squeeze out each clove
8. Either use in a recipe or spread directly on bread

Hummus

This is great for dipping chopped vegetables, tortilla chips or breadsticks in. You can make it more interesting with the addition of roasted tomato, peppers or chilies.

Ingredients:
- 15oz can chickpeas (drained and rinsed)
- ¼ cup fresh lemon juice (approximately one large lemon)
- ¼ cup tahini
- 1 minced garlic clove (small)
- 2-3 tablespoons water
- 2 tablespoons extra-virgin olive oil (more needed to serve)
- ½ teaspoon ground cumin
- Salt to taste

Method:
1. Add the lemon juice and tahini in to your food processor and blend for 1 minute
2. Scrape down the sides and blend again for another 30 seconds
3. Add the cumin, ½ teaspoon salt, minced garlic and olive oil and

blend for another 30 seconds
4. Scrape down the sides and bottom, then blend for another 30-40 seconds until thoroughly combined
5. Add half the chickpeas and blend for another minute
6. Scrape the sides and bottom, add the rest of the chickpeas and blend for another minute or two until smooth but thick
7. If it is too thick or not smooth enough, add water, a tablespoon at a time, and blend until you get the perfect consistency
8. Taste, and add salt if necessary
9. Serve with a dash of paprika and a drizzle of olive oil
10. This will store for about a week in an airtight contain in your refrigerator

Roasted Garlic and Tomato Sauce

This is a fantastic sauce to use in any Italian dish or even to top a pizza!

Ingredients:

- 16oz jar roasted red bell peppers
- 6 small tomatoes
- 1 head of garlic
- ¼ cup water
- 5 tablespoons extra virgin olive oil (divided)
- 1 tablespoon fresh basil (chopped)
- 1 teaspoon dried red pepper flakes
- Salt and pepper to taste

Method:

1. Preheat your oven to 450F
2. Put the whole head of garlic (unpeeled) in an over-proof dish
3. Drizzle a tablespoon of olive oil over it and add ¼ cup water
4. Roast for around 45 minutes
5. Purée the tomatoes in your blender
6. Drain the bell peppers and add to the food processor, blending until pureed
7. Carefully remove five cloves from the head and squeeze them into the blender
8. Add 4 tablespoons olive oil and blend for a few seconds
9. Add the basil and red pepper flakes, seasoning with salt and pepper to taste
10. Blend again until it achieves the desired consistency
11. Use immediately or refrigerate and use within a couple of days

Garlic Green Beans

This is a great way to serve fresh green beans, and the same can be done to broccoli and asparagus, to make for an interesting side dish.

Ingredients:

- 2 x 14½oz cans green beans (drained – or fresh green beans)
- 1 medium sized head of garlic (peeled and sliced)
- ¼ cup Parmesan cheese (grated)
- 3 tablespoons extra virgin olive oil
- 1 tablespoon butter
- Salt and pepper to taste

Method:

1. Melt the butter in a large skillet on a medium heat
2. Add the olive oil to the butter and heat
3. Add the garlic and cook, stirring frequently, until lightly browned
4. Stir in the green beans and season to taste
5. Cook for a further 10 minutes until the beans are tender
6. Remove from the heat, sprinkle the cheese over the top and serve

Other Members of the Onion Family

Although garlic is a lovely vegetable, there are other members of the same family which are delicious. In this section, you will learn about some of the other popular members of this family, including the rather lovely ornamental onions, which have beautiful flowers.

Leeks

Leeks have a lovely, mild onion flavor and are ideal for stews. The best part of the leek is the white stem, which comes from the stalk being out of direct sunlight. This is done either by earthing up your leeks as they are growing or growing your leeks in plastic pipes. This maximizes the white area of the leeks and ensures you get a good crop. Many people do not plant their leeks deep enough and then do not end up with enough of the white area to make the leeks worthwhile.

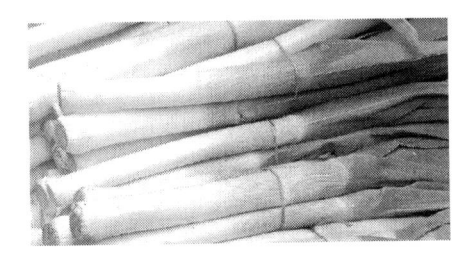

Leeks like to grow in a well-drained soil in a sunny but sheltered area. They take a long time to mature, but are worth it. Prepare the soil in winter, ready for planting in the spring, working in a lot of well-rotted manure. It does need a lot of food, so ensure the soil is well fertilized before sowing.

Most people will sow the seeds direct to the soil in either March or April, depending on the weather. I personally start mine in pots in an unheated greenhouse in late February or early March and then plant them out when they are about 4 or 5 inches high. I just scatter the seeds on the soil and then separate them when I plant them out. Leeks are fairly hardy and don't mind you messing with their roots.

Leeks are best planted about a foot (30cm) apart, because you need plenty of air circulation between the plants to prevent fungal infections. The seeds are planted about ½" (1cm) deep, covered with soil and then watered in. As the leek grows, earth up around the stem so that you get the blanched stem you are after.

Water well in dry spells and the leeks should be ready to harvest from late summer through to winter, depending on the variety.

Leeks are not keen on competition so you need to keep the weeds down, but you need to be careful not to remove sprouting leeks! They look very similar to grass and is very easy to accidentally dig them up, thinking you are getting rid of weeds. Clearly mark the rows you are planting in and leave the markers in place until the leeks are up and recognizable.

Some of my favorite varieties of leeks are:

- Musselburgh – a very popular variety, often found in stores which is winter hardy, ready to pick from December all the way through to April.
- Pandora- has lovely long white stems and is harvested from September through to January.
- Monstruoso de Carentan – a heritage leek which has shorter stems and harvests from October to January.

Remember to grow leeks in plastic tubes (make sure there is plenty of room for them to expand) in order to get nice long, white stems. This year I'm rather excited to grow some giant leek varieties, so will be posting updates on progress with these new, giant leeks on my website , which you can find at www.OwningAnAllotment.com.

Leek and Potato Soup Recipe
This is one of my favorite recipes from the allotment. With fresh leeks and potatoes, it is absolutely delicious and best of all, it is virtually fat free, so is great for anyone on a diet.

Ingredients:
- 1½lbs potatoes (peeled and finely diced)
- 2 bay leaves
- 1 large onion (peeled and finely chopped)
- 1 large leek (trimmed and shredded)
- 5¼oz fat free fromage frais
- 5 cups vegetable stock (chicken stock can be used if preferred)
- 2 tablespoons fresh chives (chopped)
- Salt and pepper to taste

Method:
1. Put the onion, bay leaves and ½ cup stock in to a large saucepan
2. Bring to the boil, cover then simmer for 5 minutes
3. Add the potato and leek to the pot (you can keen some of the shreds for decoration late)
4. Pour in the rest of the stock and season to taste
5. Return to the boil, cover and simmer for 25 to 30 minutes until tender
6. Remove the bay leaves
7. Blend the mixture – either use a stick blender or transfer to a food processor
8. Return to the saucepan and stir in the fromage frais without boiling
9. Serve sprinkled with shredded leek, chopped chives and freshly ground black pepper

Onions

There are a lot of different types of onion, from pickling onions which are smaller to Spanish onions, red onions, white onions and even mammoth onions, which all require very similar growing conditions. Some are grown from sets (very small onions) and others are grown seeds. The more common and popular varieties are grown from sets, but the more unusual varieties are grown from seeds.

Onion sets are basically immature onions that are planted in the spring or towards the end of summer. Each one will form a full-sized bulb when it is ready to harvest. The best onion sets to buy are heat treated ones, which are less likely to bolt.

Growing from sets is much easier than growing from seed, as onions can be tricky to get going from seed, particularly in cooler or damper areas.

Onions grow best in a sunny, well-drained location. Although they will grow in a heavy soil, you need to improve the drainage to prevent the onions rotting. Alternatively, if you have a heavy soil, plant your onion sets in 4" high ridges of soil, which will help stop moisture building up in the soil.

Onions like a good, fertile soil, but they do not need high levels of nitrogen. They don't appreciate being planted in freshly matured soil. If you are digging in manure, do it a few months before planting so that it has time to rot down. Onions prefer a slightly alkaline soil, so if yours is acidic, lime it to bring the pH down before planting.

Onion seeds are typically sown in January or February at a temperature of between 10-15C or 50-59F. They are sown in modules, with around half a dozen seeds in each module. You can either separate out the seedlings when you plant out or the bulbs will just push themselves apart as they grow.

Sow your seeds in the spring for an August harvest and then sow again in late summer for onions ready from around June the following year. The longer you leave onions in the ground, the bigger they will grow, but be careful they do not get waterlogged and rot.

Sets are planted with the pointy end (neck) just poking up above the soil. They should be weeded regularly and watered occasionally. Weeds will very quickly swamp onions so it is vital that you keep the weeds down. Watch out for them sending up flower stalks and remove any of these that you see as they will reduce the size of the bulb.

Onions are ready to harvest when the foliage begins to turn yellow and wilt. They are then pulled up and dried. The bulbs need to be laid out, with foliage and roots intact in a dry, warm area for about two weeks to dry out. Any onions with thick necks should be used quickly as they will not dry out and store.

When the foliage is completely dry the onions can be stored somewhere cool and dry where they will last for 3 to 6 months. Hang the onions in nets or plait them, like you would garlic. Personally, I hang them in lady's tights (pantyhose) by cutting the foliage and roots off, putting an onion in a leg then tying a knot above it. The next onion is put in, then another knot tied and the process repeated until the leg is full of onions. Then it is hung and onions are cut out from the bottom up until they are all used.

Onions are very easy to grow and you can grow some lovely varieties at home. It is easy to grow enough onions for most of the year if they are well stored and they are a low maintenance crop.

Shallots

Shallots are a gourmet onion, very sought after in cooking because it has a much milder flavor than onions and stores better, anything from 12 to 18 months. There are a lot of varieties of shallot and there is a difference in taste between the different varieties. Although you can grow shallots from seed, most people start them off from sets which are much easier to grow. A single set will produce anywhere from four to nine full sized shallots.

Growing conditions for shallots are very similar to onions, a good, well-drained soil that is not too high in nitrogen, but is fertile. Like onions they do best in a slightly alkaline soil, but will tolerate acidic conditions.

Traditionally, shallots are planted on the shortest day for harvesting on the longest, though most of us plant them at the end of January to early February, though they will tolerate being planted as late as March! They are typically harvested from June through to August.

Sets are planted about 4-5" (10-12cm) apart, with 8" (20cm) between rows. They are planted in exactly the same way as onions, with the neck of the bulb just breaking through the surface.

These are a low maintenance crop and once planted there is not much for you to do except keep the weeds down (shallots don't like competition) and water occasionally during dry spells.

Shallots suffer from many similar problems to onions, though they do not bolt as often nor do they often suffer from rust. Probably the biggest problem, like onions, is birds pulling newly planted sets out of the ground. If this is an issue you may want to cover the sets until they are established.

Shallots are harvested by gently lifting them with a fork. They are loose in the soil when ready and once picked you can split them or leave them together (they dry better when split).

The shallots need to be dried for a couple of weeks before the foliage and roots removed and they are hung like onions. Often shallots are tied in bunches before being hung to dry. Shallots will store for anything between 12 and 18 months in the right conditions.

There are three main types of shallot, yellow, red and French Jersey, which have a more elongated shape, though may not store as well.

This type of onion is great to use in cooking and has a very nice flavor. With such a long shelf life, they are ideal to use when your onion crop has been used up and you are waiting for the next harvest.

Ornamental Onion Varieties

As well as the edible varieties of onion there are ornamental varieties which are grown for the flowers. They come in a wide variety of sizes and colors ranging from blue to purple to white and yellow. They tend to be tall plants and make for a very striking display, even looking good when the plant dies back and the flower dries. There are shorter versions of alliums available.

Ornamental alliums do no appreciate the cold, do not like to be exposed to the elements and hate being waterlogged. They should not be planted in a freshly manured soil either. They like a sheltered position in the sun with well-drained soil.

Bulbs are planted in the fall to a depth of four times the bulb's diameter. Smaller alliums are usually planted 3-4" apart whilst the taller ones will need as much as 8" between bulbs. They will also grow well in deep containers, but make sure you water during dry spells and replace the compost every year.

Although alliums have lovely flowers, the foliage is a bit straggly so you will often plant alliums behind other plants so their leaves are hidden. Once the flowers have died down, you can lift, divide and replant clumps of alliums to give them more space to grow.

These ornamental onions suffer from many of the same problems as their edible cousins, but are usually trouble free when grown in a border. Most problems come from the bulbs not being planted deep enough or the soil not being of the right type.

There are lots of varieties of flowering allium on the market and you are best to browse through a seed catalog to determine which ones you like. You can find them in garden centers, but your selection will be limited. There are some fantastic varieties out there, and alliums make for a superb addition to any flower bed with eye catching flowers that grab attention.

ENDNOTE

Garlic is a fantastic vegetable to grow and is surprisingly easy to succeed with. It is very forgiving of conditions and doesn't mind neglect but will get crowded out by weeds if you are not careful. Probably the main cause of garlic crop failure is because they are killed off by the faster growing weeds.

Choosing the right variety to grow is very important as there are a lot of different types of garlic on the market. Which you choose will depend on where you are in the world, as some garlics tolerate colder climates than others, and what you are planning on using your garlic for.

Whether you plant in the fall or spring is up to you. If your winters are cold and dry then fall planting works well, though in areas with damp and cool winters, spring planting is often better to avoid fungal diseases.

With just a few bulbs you can easily grow enough garlic to supply you for the entire year as some varieties will store well. You much be careful not to leave the garlic in the ground too long as it can become overripe, which makes the bulb split and the individual cloves start to send up shoots. Harvested, dried and cured, it will last for plenty of time.

As well as the traditional types of garlic, some people like elephant garlic, which is actually a type of leek, rather than garlic. It has a much milder flavor, and with its large size, is ideal for roasting.

How you use your garlic is entirely up to you. Mine is added to meals for flavor, but some people grow it for its health benefits. It is a plant that has a huge range of therapeutic uses, so many people deliberately eat raw garlic because of this. Whilst it does have a lot of health benefits, it does make you smell when you eat too much. Not only does your breath smell, but you also sweat garlic if you eat too much. For most people, using it in normal cooking is enough and will give you the majority of the health benefits.

Although garlic does have its fair share of problems, most of the time you will have no issues at all, providing you plant the bulbs in the right type of soil, well spaced and keep them free from weeds. Garlic leaves are tall and narrow, so they don't crowd out weeds like many other plants do. Unfortunately, weeds will crowd out your garlic, causing poor air circulation and increasing the risk of fungal diseases such as rust.

Growing your own garlic is very easy to do and even a single bulb is enough to supply you with plenty of garlic for the year. It doesn't take up a lot of space, doesn't have deep roots and can be planted in between other crops or plants. It can help to keep bugs off many plants and is a great companion plant for a wide variety of plants, though there are a few which do not like garlic near it.

Anyone can grow their own garlic at home and enjoy the many benefits of this fantastic plant. Go out and buy some seed bulbs (don't use supermarket bulbs as you don't know if they are disease free) and plant them at the right time of year. This is a great opportunity to try some of the more unusual, and delicious varieties of garlic, including elephant garlic which you are bound to love!

About Jason

Jason has been a keen gardener for over twenty years, having taken on numerous weed infested patches and turned them into productive vegetable gardens.

One of his first gardening experiences was digging over a 400 square foot garden in its entirety and turning it into a vegetable garden, much to the delight of his neighbors who all got free vegetables! It was through this experience that he discovered his love of gardening and started to learn more and more about the subject.

His first encounter with a greenhouse resulted in a tomato infested greenhouse but he soon learnt how to make the most of a greenhouse and now grows a wide variety of plants from grapes to squashes to tomatoes and more. Of course, his wife is delighted with his greenhouse as it means the windowsills in the house are no longer filled with seed trays every spring.

He is passionate about helping people learn to grow their own fresh produce and enjoy the many benefits that come with it, from the exercise of gardening to the nutrition of freshly picked produce. He often says that when you've tasted a freshly picked tomato you'll never want to buy another one from a store again!

Jason is also very active in the personal development community, having written books on self-help, including subjects such as motivation and confidence. He has also recorded over 80 hypnosis programs, being a fully qualified clinical hypnotist which he sells from his website www.MusicForChange.com.

He hopes that this book has been a pleasure for you to read and that you have learned a lot about the subject and welcomes your feedback either directly or through an Amazon review. This feedback is used to improve his books and provide better quality information for his readers.

Jason also loves to grow giant and unusual vegetables and is still planning on breaking the 400lb barrier with a giant pumpkin. He hopes that with his new allotment plot he'll be able to grow even more exciting vegetables to share with his readers.

OTHER BOOKS BY JASON

Please check out my other gardening books on Amazon, available on Kindle and paperback.

Container Gardening - Growing Vegetables, Herbs & Flowers in Containers
A step by step guide showing you how to create your very own container garden. Whether you have no garden, little space or you want to grow specific plants, this book guides you through everything you need to know about planting a container garden from the different types of pots, to which plants thrive in containers to handy tips helping you avoid the common mistakes people make with containers.

Greenhouse Gardening - A Beginners Guide To Growing Fruit and Vegetables All Year Round
A complete, step by step guide to owning your own greenhouse. Learn everything you need to know from sourcing greenhouses to building foundations to ensuring it survives high winds. This handy guide will teach you everything you need to know to grow a wide range of plants in your greenhouse, including tomatoes, chilies, squashes, zucchini and much more. Find out how you can benefit from a greenhouse today, they are more fun and less work than you might think!

Growing Fruit: The Complete Guide to Growing Fruit At Home
This is a complete guide to growing fruit from apricots to walnuts and everything in between. You will learn how to choose fruit plants, how to grow and care for them, how to store and preserve the fruit and much more. With recipes, advice and tips this is the perfect book for anyone who

wants to learn more about growing fruit at home, whether beginner or experienced gardener.

Growing Giant Pumpkins – How to Grow Massive Pumpkins At Home

A complete step by step guide detailing everything you need to know to produce pumpkins weighing hundreds of pounds, if not edging into the thousands! Anyone can grow giant pumpkins at home and this book gives you the insider secrets of the giant pumpkin growers showing you how to avoid the mistakes people commonly make when trying to grow a giant pumpkin. This is a complete guide detailing everything from preparing the soil to getting the right seeds to germinating the seeds and caring for your pumpkins.

Growing Tomatoes: Your Guide To Growing Delicious Tomatoes At Home

This is the definitive guide to growing delicious and fresh tomatoes at home. Teaching you everything from selecting seeds to planting and caring for your tomatoes as well as diagnosing problems this is the ideal book for anyone who wants to grow their own tomatoes. You will learn the secrets of a successful tomato grower and learn about the many different types of tomato you could grow, most of which are not available in any shops! A comprehensive must have guide.

How to Compost – Turn Your Waste into Brown Gold

This is a complete step by step guide to making your own compost at home. Vital to any gardener, this book will explain everything from setting up your compost heap to how to ensure you get fresh compost in just a few weeks. You will learn the techniques for producing highly nutritious compost that will help your plants grow whilst recycling your kitchen waste. A must have handbook for any gardener who wants their plants to benefit from home-made compost.

How To Grow Potatoes - The Guide To Choosing, Planting and Growing in Containers Or the Ground

Learn everything you need to know about growing potatoes at home. Discover the wide variety of potatoes you can grow, many delicious varieties you will never see in the shops. Find out the best way to grow potatoes at home, how to protect your plants from the many pests and diseases and how to store your harvest so you can enjoy fresh potatoes over winter. A complete step by step guide telling you everything you need to know to successfully grow potatoes at home.

Hydroponics: A Beginners Guide to Growing Food without Soil

Hydroponics is growing plants without soil, which is a fantastic idea for indoor gardens. It is surprisingly easy to set up, once you know what you are doing, and is significantly more productive and quicker than growing in soil. It doesn't even have to be expensive to get started and the possibilities are endless. This book will tell you everything you need to know to get started growing flowers, vegetables and fruit hydroponically at home.

Raised Bed Gardening – A Guide To Growing Vegetables In Raised Beds

Learn why raised beds are such an efficient and effortless way to garden as you discover the benefits of no-dig gardening, denser planting and less bending, ideal for anyone who hates weeding or suffers from back pain. Easy to build and lasting for years I cannot recommend this method of gardening enough for its many benefits! You will learn everything you need to know to build your own raised beds, plant them and ensure they are highly productive.

Square Foot Gardening – Growing More In Less Space

Learn about this unique gardening style which enables you to grow more in less space. This dense planting method using nutrient rich soil to produce fantastic yields. You will learn exactly how to create your own square foot garden, how to create the perfect soil mix and exactly how to space your plants for maximum yields. You will find out what you can grow in a square foot garden as well as what to avoid growing plus helpful advice so you can make the most of your growing area. An in-depth guide to get you started with your first square foot garden.

Straw Bale Gardening – No Dig, No Bending Productive Vegetable Gardens

This book tells you everything you want to know about the innovative method of straw bale gardening. Discover this no dig, no bend, low maintenance form of growing fruits, vegetables and flowers that is gaining a lot of attention. Very productive and a great alternative to raised bed gardens, this book will guide you through the whole process from setting up your bales to planting and more. A complete, step by step guide to this innovating gardening method.

Vertical Gardening: Maximum Productivity, Minimum Space

This is exciting form of gardening allows you to grow large amounts of fruit and vegetables in small areas, maximizing your usage of space. Whether you have a large garden, an allotment or just a small balcony, you will be able to grow more delicious fresh produce. Becoming more popular not just amongst gardeners but even with city planners, this is a fantastic gardening technique that significantly boost your yield. Find out how I grew over 70 strawberry plants in just three feet of ground space and more in this detailed guide.

Worm Farming – Creating Compost at Home with Vermiculture
An in-depth guide to one of the hottest topics on the market as you learn how you can use worms to turn your kitchen scraps into a high quality, highly nutritious compost that will help your plants to thrive! Easy to set up, low cost and able to be done in a small corner of a shed or garage this is a fantastic way for anyone to make their own compost or even scale it up to create a highly profitable business. Discover how you can make one of the best composts on the market with kitchen waste and worms!

Want More Inspiring Gardening Ideas?

This book is part of the Inspiring Gardening Ideas series. Bringing you the best books anywhere on how to get the most from your garden or allotment.

You can find out about more wonderful books just like this one at: www.OwningAnAllotment.com

Follow me at www.YouTube.com/OwningAnAllotment for my video diary and tips. Join me on Facebook for regular updates and discussions at www.Facebook.com/OwningAnAllotment.

If you sign up for my free newsletter, you will be notified of all of my new books coming out and even how to get many of them for free. Plus, you will get coupons good for 20% off any of the training that is offered by myself.

Thank you for reading!

Printed in Great Britain
by Amazon